DO NOT REMOVE
CARDS FROM POCKET

Black Writers / Black Baseball

Black Writers /
Black Baseball

*An Anthology of Articles
from Black Sportswriters
Who Covered the Negro Leagues*

by JIM REISLER

with a foreword by DON NEWCOMBE

McFarland & Company, Inc., Publishers
Jefferson, North Carolina, and London

British Library Cataloguing-in-Publication data are available

Library of Congress Cataloguing-in-Publication Data

Reisler, Jim, 1958–
    Black writers/black baseball : an anthology of articles from Black
sportswriters who covered the Negro leagues / by Jim Reisler.
      p. cm.
    Includes index.
    ISBN 0-7864-0002-1 (lib. bdg.: 50# alk. paper) ∞
    1. Sportswriters—United States—Biography. 2. Afro-American
journalists—Biography. 3. Negro leagues—History. I. Title.
GV742.4.R45 1994
070.4'49796'092—dc20
[B]   94-6936
                                               CIP

Manufactured in the United States of America

McFarland & Company, Inc., Publishers
 Box 611, Jefferson, North Carolina 28640

For Tobie, who understands,
and for Julia, who no doubt will

ACKNOWLEDGMENTS

This project started on a sweltering August afternoon in 1991, the kind of day made for baseball. Precisely 27 trips to Harlem's Schomburg Center for Research in Black Culture and countless letters and telephone calls later, it is complete and there are several people to thank.

First and foremost my gratitude goes to the two living representatives of this group of pioneer journalists, Sam Lacy of *The Baltimore Afro-American* and Ed Harris, formerly of *The Philadelphia Tribune*. Both were gracious in their time and memories.

I offer my thanks as well to several children of the represented writers—Lee Bostic, son of Joe Bostic, Douglas Washington, son of Chester L. Washington, and D'Anne Burley, daughter of Dan Burley—for supplying biographical information and photos.

I am grateful also to Lois Walker of *The Chicago Defender* for her help in securing photos of Frank Young and Wendell Smith; to Don Newcombe of the Dodgers for penning a foreword to this book; to Steve Spencer for his artwork; and to Dick Clark of the Society for American Baseball Research for his support.

Special thanks go to my wife, Tobie, and daughter, Julia, for their patience and understanding.

Jim Reisler
Irvington, N.Y.
October 1993

CONTENTS

FOREWORD

As a young ballplayer with the Negro leagues' Newark Eagles, I never in my wildest dreams thought that future generations of baseball fans would give much thought to our performance on the field.

Happily, I was wrong, for today, interest in the Negro leagues is greater than ever. Thanks, in part, to the work of writers and historians, the exploits of my peers—great black players like Cool Papa Bell, Satchel Paige and Jackie Robinson—are being properly acknowledged.

In this book the words of eight great black baseball–beat writers who covered us recreate the feel and texture of life in the Negro leagues. Men like Sam Lacy, Wendell Smith, Dan Burley and Joe Bostic form an important but little known part of baseball history that is well worth remembering.

So much has happened since those long ago but history making times. With Jackie Robinson paving the way, several of us who played in the Negro leagues made it to stardom in the major leagues. As one of the fortunate ones who made it, I look back with pride at all that we early black major league players accomplished.

What a shame then that the writers whose work appears on these pages haven't yet received their rightful due. These are men, more of whom deserve their place, specifically in the Writers' Wing at the Baseball Hall of Fame in Cooperstown.

May this volume be a solid push in the right direction.

Don Newcombe
Newark Eagles & Brooklyn Dodgers

INTRODUCTION

Forgotten Voices

Before Dwight Gooden, there was Satchel Paige. Long before Kirby Puckett and Ricky Henderson were Rube Foster, Josh Gibson and Oscar Charleston. They were baseball players before their time, star athletes from the 1920s, '30s and '40s who belonged in the major leagues but were excluded because they were black.

"The greatest team I ever saw?" asked Baseball Hall of Famer Buck Leonard, a former member of the Homestead Grays and a legend of his time. "The 1936 Pittsburgh Crawfords. No doubt about it. Why, any one of those ballplayers could have made the major leagues."

But only one—Satchel Paige—actually did. Instead, these black ballplayers, playing on teams like the Crawfords and the Grays, formed their own leagues, the "Negro leagues." There, until a few years after Jackie Robinson finally reached the major leagues in 1947, baseball behind the color barrier flourished, often providing more excitement than was to be found in the white major leagues. There were World Series, All-Star games, rivalries, packed ballparks, exaggerated headlines and, most of all, ballplayers of fabulous talent.

Only recently has recognition come to this group of marvelous ballplayers. Ten men who spent their entire careers on Negro league teams have, since 1971, been enshrined in the Hall of Fame. But as the ballplayers themselves gain well-deserved recognition, there is a further group of sportsmen from the era who also deserve our attention. The men who covered these ballplayers—the black baseball writers—are pioneers in their own right.

This is an anthology of pieces by the newspaper reporters whose job was covering the Negro leagues. These forgotten giants of black journalism include Frank Young of *The Chicago Defender*, the first full-time black sportswriter and the dean of his trade; Dr. W. Rollo Wilson of *The Pittsburgh Courier* and *The Philadelphia Tribune*, a pharmacist by trade and the Red Smith of his day; Sam Lacy of *The Baltimore Afro-American*, still at it

1

after all these years; Joe Bostic of *The People's Voice* of Harlem; Ed Harris of *The Philadelphia Tribune;* and *The Courier*'s Wendell Smith, generally acknowledged as the best black sportswriter of his generation and recently enshrined in the Writers' Wing of the Hall of Fame.

Others, like Dan Burley of *The Amsterdam News* and Chester "Ches" Washington of *The Courier,* also wrote eloquently about baseball, but became better known later on for other things — Burley as an author, musician and staff writer for *Ebony,* and Washington as the proprietor of a modern-day media empire, the Los Angeles–based Wave Newspaper Group. But it just may have been their work as baseball writers in which they achieved their most lasting influence.

All worked for weekly black newspapers, most of which operated on shoestring budgets, despite large circulations and enduring importance in the black community. They wrote long before television, when newspapers were still the primary means of communication. "We had influence because people just read more back then," said Sam Lacy, one of only two writers in the group still living (Ed Harris is the other). "It was that simple." Indeed, *The Courier* at one time had the largest circulation of any black paper in the country — close to 300,000 — with readership stretching far into the South.

They were extraordinary men. Jackie Robinson said that he could never have made it to the major leagues without Smith's help. Indeed, their most lasting collective contribution may have been an eloquent, persistent and occasionally bitter demonstration of words designed to urge the white baseball establishment to integrate. It was that same group who actively accompanied black players to tryouts with major league teams, making their case face-to-face with the white owners. Arguably, their campaign was what finally pushed big league owners to question and finally end the color ban.

They also were renaissance men. Of the eight, six went to college, an extraordinary number in an era when it was unusual for journalists — let alone sports journalists — to pursue an education beyond high school. Several wrote books. Others wrote their paper's weekly entertainment column, or worked as city editor. That several were better known for accomplishments other than their sports writing is indicative of the extraordinary collective range of their talents.

"At a time when few whites thought of racial issues, these writers injected the integration controversy not only into the black press, but into the broader public arena," writes historian Jules Tygiel in *Baseball's Great Experiment,* his superb 1983 chronicle of Jackie Robinson's entry into the major leagues. Indeed, reading their work is to plunge into the day-to-day happenings of a rich baseball past.

Here, for instance, is Rollo Wilson's 1930 profile of Josh Gibson as an awkward teenager who might be good enough to make the team. Some 17 years and 900-plus home runs later, here is the same Gibson, presented in a Wilson column as broken down, injured and near the end of a career cut short by sickness and personal problems.

There is gushing prose generated by black baseball's biggest spectacle, the annual East-West All-Star Game in Chicago, which drew upwards of 50,000 spectators each year. There are hometown profiles of Satchel Paige and Jackie Robinson—among the first newspaper coverage of these men—and there is day-to-day coverage of a multidue of long forgotten Negro league baseball issues: unscrupulous owners, rowdy fans, the lack of cohesive leagues, players jumping to Mexico, and yes, underpaid ball-players.

Here as well is the evolution of the sports column revealed. Newspaper reporters did not write sports columns much until the mid–1920s or so, when Frank Young and Chester Washington were among the first to take up the practice on a regular basis. Although Young joined *The Defender* in 1906, he and other writers generally limited their baseball coverage to bland, longish game summaries, with the occasional analysis sounding more like summaries of military strategy and few, if any, player or manager profiles or quotes. By the early 1930s, however, that had started to change, as columnists discovered colorful personalities like Satchel Paige and James Bell, the man known as "Cool Papa." With the influx of younger writers like Smith, Lacy and Harris in the middle to late 1930s, the maturation of the baseball column was complete.

Covering the Negro leagues carried its own peculiar set of problems. Take the well-documented barnstorming aspect of the Negro league game, the scheduling of which made it impractical for the weekly papers to send writers with the teams. Relegated to the back alleys of the sports world, black teams played on—"every day in a different town, sometimes three games a day," said Buck Leonard. Crisscrossing the country in their trademark overcrowded buses, black teams took on all comers, from sand-lot and mill teams to the professional black teams in their own loosely structured leagues. In 1938 alone, the Homestead Grays played 210 games and traveled 30,000 miles. For their 80 or so home games, the Grays used Forbes Field, the Pittsburgh Pirates' ballpark. But they dressed at the local Y.M.C.A., with the ballpark locker rooms off limits.

When the writers traveled, they were subject to the same racial prejudice as the players. "They had white hotels and white restaurants," said Leonard, from his home in Rocky Mount, North Carolina. "They had buses and we had to sit in the back. But it was something we'd been living with our whole lives, and baseball was only part of it. Our time hadn't come."

Sam Lacy mirrors those words, with his story of how he was barred from press boxes all over the South. His columns of traveling with Jackie Robinson and the Brooklyn Dodgers tell of one rat-trap, flea-bag hotel after another, all, of course, across town from the hotel housing the white players.

"The efforts of [black writers] to integrate sports possessed an element of irony," writes Tygiel in *Baseball's Great Experiment*. "They too were victims of Jim Crow, who held analogous positions to the athletes they covered. Segregation hid their considerable skills from the larger white audience and severely restricted their income earning potential. Yet they rarely mentioned their own plight. Indeed, the barriers for black journalists lasted long after those for athletes disappeared."

The barnstorming aspect of the game limited the Negro league schedule to only 50 or so league games a season, skewing the statistics. For instance, Leonard, who spent his entire 17-year career with the Grays, had his best year in 1939-40, when he batted no lower than .390 and possibly as high as .492. And although Josh Gibson, the home run king of black baseball, is credited with hitting 972 home runs during his 17-year career, no one knows how many of those home runs came against sandlot teams or inferior pitching—all of which left black newspapers in a quandary about the coverage. Even so, said Negro league star and Hall of Famer Judy Johnson, a few months before his death in 1991, "Josh was the greatest hitter I ever saw, the absolute greatest."

Black sportswriters had to be versatile. Because most black papers operated on slim budgets and even slimmer staffs, sportswriters were routinely pulled off their regular beats to cover other stories. Wendell Smith, for instance, was simultaneously *The Pittsburgh Courier*'s city editor, assistant sports editor and sports columnist, while Dan Burley wrote sports and entertainment columns for *The Amsterdam News*. "It meant you had to be aggressive and know a little about everything," says Sam Lacy. "By working for small papers with small staffs, we also covered other beats that took us beyond just sports or baseball. We had to be well-rounded writers."

Typically, said Lacy, a black newspaper's sports department consisted of two or three men, a couple of typewriters and a desk or two in a corner of the newsroom. Ed Harris reported even more severe conditions: "I was the sports department." Still, they turned out an enormous volume of baseball coverage right on cue each April through October. Lacy again: "You just did the best you could, but it could be tough."

Of the 445 known games played between black and white teams played from 1886 to 1948, Negro league teams won 269, lost 172 and tied 4. Said Philadelphia A's owner Connie Mack of Judy Johnson: "If he were white, he could name his price." Johnson added, "We were better than many of the players today; now, the pitchers go nine innings and need four days off. Ours would go nine, and pitch the next day, too."

Although a few black players were permitted to play on early white professional teams, their presence was not welcome. The first black professional teams appeared in the 1880s, concentrated mostly in the New York and Philadelphia areas. Early powerhouse teams included the Cuban Giants, the Cuban X Giants, the Philadelphia Giants and the Chicago Unions. The name "Giants" was widely popular at the time because of the popularity of the New York National League team of that name.

The first successful formation of a black professional league was in 1920, when Rube Foster organized the Negro National League. The Eastern Colored League formed three years later. From 1924 to 1927, the two leagues met in a World Series. The Negro American League was born in 1929, and along with the Negro National League, continued into the early 1950s.

Inevitably, the breaking of the white leagues' color line in 1947 spelled the beginning of the end for Negro baseball. With black fans turning their attention to the exploits of Jackie Robinson, and with major league clubs starting to raid Negro league rosters for talent with no compensation, black baseball quickly lost its allure.

It was October 1945 when Dodgers' general manager Branch Rickey signed Robinson, who had just completed his first and only season in the Negro leagues with the Kansas City Monarchs. What happened to break baseball's long racial barrier? Most significant may have been the death of Commissioner Kenesaw Mountain Landis, who had strictly policed the color line in his more than two decades as the dictatorial czar of baseball. So firm was Landis' grip on baseball owners that he quietly but decisively vetoed a plan in 1943 by young Bill Veeck to buy the Philadelphia Phillies and stock the team with Negro league stars.

The case for integration got a further boost from World War II, which for many Americans exposed the true hypocrisy of racial separation. Black soldiers who faced nationwide Jim Crow regulations at army bases protested their treatment, as did black labor leader, A. Phillip Randolph, who campaigned for an end to federal job discrimination. Indeed, *The Pittsburgh Courier*'s "Double-V" campaign of the era was intended as victory abroad and a racial victory at home.

A second organization to boost the call for black players in the major leagues was the American Communist party, whose newspaper, *The Daily Worker*, habitually attacked the unfairness of the system. And by the mid–1940s, white sportswriters like Shirley Povich in Washington and Bill Roeder in New York were also extolling the virtues of black players and urging in their columns for Negro leaguers to get a chance with white teams.

Indeed, the call for integration reached a fever pitch by 1945, with some black writers adopting showmanlike, theatrical methods to change opinion. On April 6, 1945, Joe Bostic appeared at the Dodgers' Bear Mountain, New York, training camp with Negro league stars Terris McDuffie and Dave "Showboat" Thomas, and forced Rickey to hold try-outs for the two players. Ten days later, Wendell Smith, white sportswriter Dave Egan of Boston and Boston city councilman Isadore Muchnick organized an unsuccessful tryout with the Red Sox for Robinson and two other black players. As a response to these two events, major league baseball organized a Committee on Baseball Integration, but the group never met.

By then, Rickey was already scouting black players for the Dodgers, creating a complicated smokescreen in the process to obscure his efforts. In May 1945, Rickey announced the formation of a new franchise, the Brooklyn Brown Dodgers, and a new league, the United States League. Then he sent his best scouts to watch black ballplayers—ostensibly for the Brown Dodgers, but in reality for the Dodgers' National League club.

With Robinson's breakthrough, other young Negro League stars like Roy Campanella, Don Newcombe and Larry Doby, the American League's first black player, hooked on with major league clubs. Their impact was evident in the selection of the Rookie of the Year award, first presented in 1947; of the first seven National League winners, six were black.

With top young black players turning to the major leagues, so did the crowds. For Negro league baseball, the effect was devastating. Although the leagues stumbled on for a few more years, they functioned increasingly as a kind of minor league for the majors; by 1953, a scant six years after Robinson's debut, Negro league baseball was dead.

Anyone doubting the dramatic societal importance of Jackie Robinson and other early black players need only look elsewhere on the sports pages of black newspapers in the 1930s. Crowding the baseball coverage were a growing number of triumphs by other black athletes, like world heavyweight boxing champion Joe Louis and runner Jesse Owens, whose four gold medals at the 1936 Berlin Olympics and alleged snubbing by Adolph Hitler thrilled black and white Americans alike. If Louis and Owens could perform at the top of their sports, didn't blacks at least belong in the majors? Increasingly, the answer was a resounding "yes."

Weighty thoughts these were, and fascinating to read about. There is a common thread running through these pages—talented journalists pursuing their work with professionalism and a kind of folksy humor rare on today's sports page. Baseball was a refuge from the often blaring headlines in black newspapers of the day, which, in true tabloid fashion, seldom shied from the truly horrendous toll of misfortune generated by the concept of "separate but equal" and other forms of racism.

Frank Young was the first known black writer to question the hypocrisy of baseball's color barrier, writing in 1926 in *The Chicago Defender* that "the ban against Negro players in the major leagues is a silly one, and one that should be removed." The push for integration on the black papers' sports pages was a collective effort, with younger writers like Lacy and Smith picking up the beat in the late '30s and becoming more strident as time went on. They were becoming crusaders, "although we certainly never thought of ourselves that way," said Lacy. "We were doing what we thought was right; no more, no less."

In the early 1940s, the drumbeat for integration was deafening. It was World War II, and the major leagues were hurting for quality major league players, many of whom had been drafted for the service. Still white team owners held firm, often with ridiculous and insulting results. The St. Louis Browns in 1944 actually hired a one-armed outfielder named Pete Gray rather than a black ballplayer.

Leave it to a former Newark shortstop Willie Wells, quoted in a 1944 Smith column to sum up the humiliation: "I was branded a Negro in the States, and had to act accordingly. . . . Everything I did, including playing ball, was regulated by my color. . . . They wouldn't even give me a chance in the big leagues because I was a Negro, yet they accepted every other nationality under the sun."

The glaring oversight of these marvelous Negro league ballplayers is today being slowly rectified by belated recognition. Yet the writers who crusaded on their behalf are still being overlooked. Each year, the Baseball Hall of Fame's J.G. Taylor Spink Award honors a sportswriter for "meritorious contributions to baseball writing." Although 44 men have won this award, named for the founder of *The Sporting News,* only one of the writers covered in this volume—Wendell Smith—has been so honored. Perhaps this volume can be the start of a campaign to posthumously honor some of these other remarkable writers with the award.

Meanwhile, here are some hard-hitting gems of early baseball writing that modern audiences have probably never read. Here is Harris, writing about baseball with an occasional digression on his abiding passion of pork chops. Here too are poetry from Chester Washington and folksy ramblings from Young, who covered everything from Rube Foster to why journalists like barbershops. (The answer: "[It's] a good place to close your eyes and think—especially since we have a good barber and a good one who doesn't talk your head off.")

These columns are much the same: good ones that don't talk your head off.

SAM LACY

A Living Legend

The first evidence that a living legend of black sportswriting has arrived for the work day is in the cramped lobby of *The Baltimore Afro-American* offices in downtown Baltimore. It's the name listed first in the reporter's log book, as it has been most weekdays for the past 50 years.

Name: "Lacy." Time: "6:08 A.M."

Once again, Sam Lacy, living legend, pioneer and sports editor of the paper for 50 years, has beaten the rest of the staff to the office. Sign yourself in, climb the three flights of narrow stairs to the newsroom, and Sam Lacy, dean of black sportswriters, is standing by his battered desk with a warm greeting.

At 90, Lacy is living history, a man who has won enough awards in his long career in journalism to fill a museum wing, but he still makes the trek three times a week to work from his home in southeast Washington, D.C. As for the question everyone asks him—Why do you still do it after all these years?—Lacy shrugs. "I just never thought I'd reach the stage where people were coming up and asking questions like that," he says, with a slight smile.

After all, Lacy is a newspaperman, more comfortable asking questions of others. Indeed, he has a reporter's way about him, answering phone calls by barking "Lacy" and writing succinctly, with a remarkable recall for detail.

He acknowledges the irony that after a half century of covering others, he has become the story himself. "I never thought of myself as a pioneer," he says. "It was just a case of doing what I thought was right."

Doing what he thought was right meant tireless editorial campaigning for an end to the major league color ban. He was one of the first black sportswriters to push actively for baseball integration and the first black member, in 1948, of the Baseball Writers Association of America.

Even as the major leagues were integrated, Lacy used his column in *The Afro-American* as a bully pulpit to rail against the injustice of racial

Sam Lacy (photo courtesy Sam Lacy).

inequality. "Back in the Land of Make Believe,"he wrote from St. Louis on May 5, 1948, where he was traveling with Jackie Robinson and the Brooklyn Dodgers. "Only this is no fable or fairy tale, this is Dixie, U.S.A., where they sing the 'Star-Spangled Banner' with their tongues in their cheeks, where they cry for their constitutional rights, and cry when you ask for yours, where they send the white players of the Brooklyn Dodgers to one end of town and the colored players to the other. This is the Land of Make Believe, where they sing Democratic hymns from Hitler mouths."

Lacy's reports from spring training camp are more than good, solid reporting. Their hard-hitting but honest style spared no one and achieved in the process a special poignancy.

"This is a small town in the hinterlands of deepest Texas," wrote Lacy from Texarkana, Texas. "And, in keeping with practice in Texas, white taxicabs refuse to haul colored passengers. . . . Anyway, last week when the Cleveland Indians were in town with their three colored stars, Larry Doby, Satchel Paige and Orestes Minoso, the taxicabs refused to haul them to the ballpark. Since there were no colored cabs available, and since the Indians were expecting them to play in the game against the New York Giants that afternoon, the players . . . walked." The players, Lacy wrote, arrived at the park 30 minutes late.

Lacy is a native of Mystic, Connecticut. As a young boy, he moved to Washington, D.C., where he often joined his father in the Jim Crow section in rightfield at the old Griffith Stadium to root for the Senators.

Later, the teenage Lacy shagged flies for Senators stars like Goose Goslin and Walter Johnson and worked as a Griffith Stadium vendor. Later, he played semi-pro baseball in and around Washington, competing against some of the stars of Negro league ball like Martin Dihigo and John Henry Lloyd.

In those days, Lacy says, big-name black players seldom questioned the major leagues' color ban. "Players in general weren't bothered by the fact that they couldn't be in the majors," he says. "It's like Redd Foxx used to say, 'I never knew I was poor because everyone around me was [poor] too.' They were satisfied with what they were doing and thought the closed society was something to be endured."

But Lacy's experience gave him a different insight. "Seeing and playing against both blacks and whites made me recognize that some of our guys played just as well as great white players like Sam Rice and Chick Gandel."

After graduation from Howard University, Lacy worked as a sports commentator for two Washington radio stations before landing at *The Washington Tribune* in 1934. There, for the next five years, he served as both sports editor and managing editor, rarely securing a byline but forming his substantial voice, strident for the times.

In 1937, Lacy walked the two and one-half blocks from the *Tribune* office to Griffith Stadium, where he met with Senators owner Clark Griffith to discuss integration. He was told in no uncertain terms to forget it because "the climate wasn't right."

"I explained that the climate would never be right if it wasn't tested," Lacy said. "Here were great black ballplayers like Josh Gibson, Buck Leonard and Cool Papa Bell coming into Griffith Stadium every Thursday and Sunday night when his team was away," Lacy said. "These players belonged in the major leagues."

Griffith also expressed to Lacy the common excuse of the day—that putting black players into the major leagues would destroy the Negro leagues. "But I said that the Negro leagues were a symbol of prejudice," said Lacy. "Griffith didn't budge. He didn't even entertain my thought."

Back at the *Tribune,* Lacy championed integration through his column. Like Wendell Smith, his versatility was considerable, with jobs as both sports editor and managing editor. And like Smith, his job at the chronically understaffed newspaper required a virtual juggling act, with baseball news competing against other stories for news space.

"In our group, you had to be aggressive and had to know a bit about everything," Lacy noted. "The average reporter in those days might cover courts in the morning, a luncheon or a ball game that afternoon, and perhaps a dinner or meeting in the evening. You had to be well-rounded because the job required you to cover everything."

Lacy focused on sports. In 1940, he moved to Chicago to work as an assistant national editor of *The Defender,* but ran into a brick wall named Frank Young and returned home in 1943 to work for the *Baltimore Afro-American.* Lacy described Young as "rather jealous of his job, a man who made a point that I was not to be writing sports."

Back home, he did, beginning his still-running weekly sports column, "A to Z." Some of his most memorable writing has filled the column. *The Afro-American* also gave Lacy the Jackie Robinson beat, which quickly became an important post. "Jackie was the best person," said Lacy. "It never crossed my mind that anyone else would have been as right. He had been in the service, played sports in the integrated atmosphere at U.C.L.A. and was a family man. He was somebody who was able to withstand the racial taunts."

Lacy and Robinson traveled together through the South, stayed in the same black hotels and shared their meals at black restaurants. Along the way, they became good friends, and endured much of the same racial bigotry and hardship of America in the 1940s. In Macon, Georgia, a cross burned on the front lawn of their boardinghouse. In Sanford, Florida, when Lacy and other black writers were turned back at the front gate, Robinson found a loose board in the outfield wall and helped the writers slip through into the ballpark.

Fortunately, Lacy found friends in several of the white baseball writers. When he was banished from watching a game from the press box roof in New Orleans, Lacy was joined by a contingent of the white writers from New York.

"Dick Young, Bill Roeder and several of the other writers said they were there to work on their tans," says Lacy. "But they were up to show me their support. They realized I wasn't one who just wanted to make a name for myself. They accepted me."

As much as Lacy supported Robinson's efforts, he also knew that once the major leagues went after black players, the end of the Negro leagues was a certainty. "I knew it would have a devastating effect on black baseball," he says today. "After Jackie, the Negro leagues was a symbol I couldn't live with anymore."

Nearly a half-century later, Lacy continues to write his column. He has covered six Olympics, worked as a sports commentator on WBAL-TV, Baltimore, and has managed to become a legend of journalism in the process. A widower, Lacy plays golf on weekends, does charity work, speaks at journalism conventions, and has earned a long list of awards, including a "Lifetime Achievement Award in Journalism" from *Sports Illustrated* in 1989, "Man of the Year" from the Pigskin Club of Washington, D.C., in 1985, four National Newspaper Writing Awards, and a 1975 induction into the Black Athletes Hall of Fame.

Leaning back in his chair, Lacy prefers to talk not about the awards, but about baseball. "Jackie Robinson was a great man, but just one story and not even the biggest story," he says. "That's because the story on blacks in the major leagues is a continuing story. We have come a long way, but we have a long way to go, a very long way."

The columns and stories that follow were originally printed in *The Baltimore Afro-American.*

June 10, 1939

"Looking 'em Over"

I umpired a couple of baseball games during the past two weeks, and, in doing so, got back closer to the sport than I have been since I stopped hopping around in the short pants and ribbed hose of the accepted diamond uniform.

There are lots of things you can see from the press box—the spectacular fielding and the sloppy bobbles, the beautiful throwing and the foolhardy base running, etc. But it's down there on the field where you rub elbows with the players on almost every play that the brilliance pleases you and the stupidity nettles you.

DY-DEE DAYS

Perhaps it's because the Old Man used to "change" me and rock me to sleep on a lullaby in which he described how Eddie Collins cut across in front of Jack Barry, snagged that peg to second and whipped it back to Wally Schang in time to thwart Washington's double-steal that afternoon.

Maybe it is due to the fact that I was a precocious weanling and was reciting "Casey at the Bat" from memory even before I'd discarded my rubber pants; it may be that it is because I cut my first tooth on a pair of sliding pads.

Probably it is the aversion to dumbness of the late Tom Payne, who broke to the saddle of upper crest baseball; or likely as not, it is due to a burning desire to see every one of their number help to prove that I'm justified in advocating the admittance of colored players to the big league game.

THE HEIGHT O' SOMETHIN'

Whatever the reason or reasons, I find myself far more painful from the display of mental dullness by our players than I am joyful over their exhibitions of mechanical stardom.

Some of the stuff I've encountered as an umpire this past fortnight would make the ghost of Rube Foster sit up and bite its chilly lip. F'rinstance:

There was the pitcher, who, with two strikes and no balls on the batter, poured the next pitch "down the middle" to be whammed out of the park for the deciding run of the game.

There was the veteran of many years of baseball who came to the plate as pinch hitter in the ninth inning, slapped the first offering down the right field foul line for a triple, only to be called out for failing to touch second base, with his team one run behind at the time.

"WHERE'S YOUR GUN?"

There was the batter who was called out for stepping across the plate to swing while he was being purposely passed. This was after he had failed to get the ball out of the infield on four previous times at bat.

There was the manager who said to me, "Gee ump, I don't mind you taking the game from us, but for gawd's sake, gimme something, won't-cha?" At the time, the score was 24–5 in favor of the opponents, and mainly because the manager and his teammates had succeeded in committing 11 errors to that point.

And there was the infield that protested the balk call on their pitcher with the following arguments:

• first baseman—"Aw man, you can't make a balk to second base."
• second baseman—"Good gracious, whatcha gonna do, let both the runners advance?"
• shortstop—"And they called Jesse James an outlaw!"
• third baseman—"A balk's a ball on the better ump. You oughta know that."

All the while, I was to them a numbskull, a robber and a thief. But—and bear all men by this witness—these were mild opinions compared to what I would have been to them had they been aware of what I was thinking. "O was some poor the Gifted gave us..."

August 12, 1939

"Sepia Stars Only Lukewarm Toward Campaign to Break Down Baseball Barriers"

Although there has been much agitation for the inclusion of colored players in major league baseball, it occurred to me recently that few people, if any, seemed to care a rap about what the players themselves think of the idea.

Newspapermen all over the country have at some time or other in the past two years, spoken out in favor of admitting qualified colored performers into the organized diamond sport. And liberal fans of both groups have raised a howl at the bars that are maintained against the potential big leaguers of the darker race.

In fact, every corner has been surveyed, every stop-gap plugged by people who sought to lend a hand in the campaign. Even major league club owners have been quoted and league presidents solicited. The leagues, from the commission on down to the players, have been canvassed for their views on the matter.

WHAT ABOUT THE PLAYERS?

But no one seems to have given a tinker's damn about the ideas of the guys they're trying to boot into the organized game.

The colored player, evidently, is big enough in the mind of the public to make top-line baseball, but too small to have any worth toward opinions on the matter.

But I remembered what a kick I got when, as a kid, I was asked how I'd like to get a bike for Christmas. And I recalled the thrill that even now never completely spends itself while I am waiting for my nightly ice cream.

Since man first became endowed with conscience and a sense of appreciation, he has felt keenly elated at the prospect of getting something. Why then, shouldn't the colored player be interrogated on the proposal to open big league ball to him, something we *think* he wants, but never bothered to *ask him* whether he does?

VIC HARRIS

Vic Harris, captain of the colored world champions, the Homestead Grays, was questioned on the proposition.

"It might be a good thing and then again, it might not be," the easy-going, soft-spoken Smoky City leader said.

"It's like this," he said. "We do have some good ballplayers among us, but not nearly as many fit for the majors as seems to be the belief. But, if they start picking them up, what are the remaining players going to do to make a living?

"Our crowds are not what they should be now. And suppose our stars—the fellows who do draw well—are gobbled up by the big clubs. How could the other 75 or 80% survive?"

JUD WILSON

A somewhat different slant was given by Jud Wilson, veteran third baseman of the Philadelphia Stars.

"Something may come from this thing in time," he said, "But I seriously doubt it. In the first place, it's too big a job for the people who are now trying to put it over. It will have to be a universal movement, and that will never be.

"It will never be, because the big league game, as it is now, is over-run with Southern blood. Fellows from the South are in the majority on almost every team in the major leagues. The New York Yankees, I believe, is about the only club made up almost entirely of players from the North, East and West.

"The training camps are in the South, the majority of minor leagues are in the South and there's a strong Southern sentiment in the stands. When the teams are on the road, these fellows would have to stop at the same hotels, eat in the same dining rooms and sleep in the same train compartments with the colored players.

"There'd be trouble for sure. And, if we were sent to other hotels or otherwise separated, the colored fans and the colored players would get hotter than they are over the present arrangement."

NAMES 13

"There are some fellows who could probably make it," Jud went on, "but at least half of them wouldn't because they are too old.

"Dick Seay, Willie Wells, Mule Suttles [Newark]; Jim West, Pat Patterson [Philadelphia Stars]; Sammy Bankhead, Josh Gibson, Buck Leonard [Homestead Grays]; Bill Wright and Sam Hughes [Elites] would have a good chance. So would Johnny Taylor, Barney Brown and Bill Perkins, now playing in Mexico.

"But you can't tell about them," Wilson concluded. "These fellows in our leagues lie too much about their ages."

FELTON SNOW

Catching a word from him between innings as he found time to sit down on the bench beside me, I got the following version from Felton Snow, manager of the Baltimore Elite Giants:

"I don't know if it would be a good thing, because we've got so many guys who just wouldn't act right. Some of these fellows who are pretty good out there on the diamond would give you a heartache elsewhere.

"You see, there are so many men who get $3 or $4 in their pockets, and right away, they want to tell 'the man' where he can go.

"We have some good players, yes. And, some of them would certainly qualify, but it is quite a task finding the right combination. Many of the good players are bad actors and many of the ordinary players are fine characters."

DICK LUNDY

Dick Lundy, regarded by many as the greatest shortstop that colored baseball has ever seen, laid the blame for lack of progress at the feet of the colored leaders themselves.

"For 25 years," Lundy said, "I have listened to them get in their meetings and lament the fact that 'colored baseball is still in its infancy, so we can't do this and we can't do that.' The result is that we're no further now than we were when the thought of organizing first came up.

"In order to get anywhere in this movement, we've got to perfect our own organization. We've got to get some men in the game with some money and who don't have to pull a lot of funny moves to cover up every little loss. It's foolish to expect to make any headway when the money is being put up by people who don't stand to lose a penny.

"With one or two of these kinds of people in colored baseball, we could adopt some hard and fast rules that would protect the organization. Then, there wouldn't be all of this jumping from one team to another and the reins could be drawn tighter all around.

"Another thing is that we haven't yet seen the advantage of keeping those of our men who know baseball in the game. Colored baseball wants to have nothing to do with a fellow after he has passed his usefulness as a player, no matter how much he knows about the game.

"If these faults are corrected and a definite publicity program arranged and followed, then perhaps colored baseball would make some headway. A strong organization of our own thus formed, it would naturally follow that we would *demand* rather than *solicit* recognition."

Colored baseball, itself, has now spoken.

August 6, 1947

"Looking 'em Over"

Muddy Ruel shifted the wad of tobacco from one side of his mouth to the other. He poked a squirt of brown into the cinders in front of the St. Louis Browns' dugout and rubbed it in with the toe spikes of his right foot.

"Yes, I can give you a frank appraisal of these two fellows," he said as he looked up at me through a pair of clear, dark brown eyes that stood out in bold relief despite a heavily sun-tanned face.

I had asked him for a candid discussion of Henry Thompson and Willard Brown, the two new Browns' rookies recently acquired from the Kansas City Monarchs.

"I can truthfully say that they've done nothing spectacular, yet neither have they done anything wrong," he said. "I can't say that they've had a fair trial as yet, but I also find it rather hard to determine just what is a 'fair trial.'

"Thommy is a fine fielder. He made two errors at the outset, before he had a chance to settle down, but he showed me enough to give me confidence in his ability to handle second base. All ballplayers make errors — that's part of the game. So you really can't hold that against him."

WANTS BROWN'S POWER

"Willard is the bigger of the two and has the greater power," continued Ruel. "He figures to be the more valuable man to use at the moment because we don't have the long ball hitter every team needs.

"Thommy is the more versatile. He can hit to all fields, can drag the ball and looks to be rather fast from the plate. He'll do us a lot of good later on, but right now, what we need more than anything else is Willard's long ball.

"I guess neither has had a thorough test. Certainly, Thommy hasn't. I had him in there when Johnny Berardino was out with a wrist injury, and he didn't do too badly. Frankly, he needs a better chance than what he's had up to now.

"Willard has been in some good spots, but hasn't been able to deliver. But, that doesn't make him a exception on this team. Nobody's delivering and that's why we're in eighth place.

"It looks like Willard can 'powder' the fast ball pitchers, but the slow stuff seems to bother him. Thommy is the same.

"I shoved Willard into the lineup and batted him sixth in the order because I figured that when he does hit, the ball will get out.

"He's got Ted Coleman's rightfield spot, not because I have given up on Ted, but because Ted has been hitting singles for his .226 average, and I felt that right now, I'd rather have a man in there who'd hit .212 with extra-basers or long-hit balls that would score us from first."

MUST LIVE WITH SELF

"In short, both of these fellows are still very much in the running for regular berths on this club. I'm watching them, of course, just as I watch every man on the team. They're no different than Vern Stephens with me. He's one of my most dependable regulars, but I keep an eye on him, watch him for mistakes and pray for him to come through in the pinch in the same way I pull for any man I have.

"Up to now, I haven't had any morale problems. I don't expect any, and certainly, I'm not looking for any. With me, and, I think, with most of our fellows, the game is the thing. I love baseball, or I wouldn't be back down here on the field. I treat it the same way I treat anything else I love." [Ruel resigned a job as Commissioner Happy Chandler's assistant to become Browns' manager.]

"I don't propose to prejudice any ballplayer who comes to me. That's how I hope to become a successful manager and that's how I intend to be able to live with myself. In fact, I don't want success any other way."

I talked with Ruel just before one of the games of the series his Browns took from the Senators in Washington. Not once during the 20 minutes he spent with me did he talk on any other plan, other than that of a thorough gentleman.

I found it hard to believe that this was the man who has gained the nickname, "Muddy," from the dirty way he used to talk to opposing players during a career that established him as one of the American League's outstanding catchers. Throughout the conversation, he never got more vulgar than "dadgummit." And, for once in lengthy term as a hard-boiled sportsman, I felt self-conscious every time I dropped a "dern" or a "darn."

But, the most refreshing aspect of the experience was the realization, afterward, that not once did Ruel hint that my interest in the Browns' rookies was based on race. Each time he referred to one of his players, he called him by first name. And, each time he spoke of Brown and Thompson, it was as though either or both were just two new men—not two colored men.

April 10, 1948

FORT WORTH, TEX.—The Brooklyn Dodgers' baseball entourage staked up Friday night on the second U.S. stop of the 1948 spring training season, and over its shoulder is Vero Beach, Fla. To the later, we bid au revoir, adios and goodbye! No auf Weidersehens, we hope!!

The place where Branch Rickey has pitched his elaborate baseball school fairly seethes with prejudice. "Dodgertown," as the Rickey brain-child is called, is an anachronism in Vero Beach. Founded on the principles of democracy and fair play, "Dodgertown" is as out of place in Vero Beach as the proverbial snowball in hell. The town, figuratively speaking, is one of those holes where they "hang out the signs" at sundown. Its citizenry is lily-white. Colored people living in the community follow the usual pattern in the south. They live together in the "colored section," but Vero Beach disowns this community and requires that it be known by another name: Gifford.

Even native Floridians, hardened to the indignities of Jim Crowism, shun Vero Beach as "a good place to be from—far away from." Despite the fact Rickey has taken a 10-year lease on a former U.S. naval station, with its own private airport, to avoid transportation problems, Vero Beach police pressed their obnoxious presence on "Dodgertown" for the two-game series between Brooklyn and the Montreal Royals last week. They had nothing to do, nobody seemed to want them around; and, with nothing to occupy them, they might have enjoyed the games. But they didn't—they busied themselves herding the colored fans into a roped-off area down the left field foul line, sweating, cussing and fuming in the process, instead of watching the game and letting others—both colored and white—do the same.

The "souvenir programs" for the Dodger-Royal games had 56 pages. Pictures of Pee Wee Reese, Carl Furillo, Bruce Edwards, etc., adorned the first pages of the booklet up to page 32. Then followed a mass of advertisements. Back on page 55, behind the ads and even behind a picture of Ed Head, who hasn't been with the Dodgers for more than a year, was a photo of Jackie Robinson... A local-born white canteen operator at Dodgertown," who was too busy to look up the price of chewing tobacco for Roy Campanella, got a verbal lashing from Brooklyn officials... His only comeback was a Mortimer Snerd grunt.

Roy Campanella lost no time finding a roommate with the Dodgers. The Bums' newest rookie moved in with Jackie Robinson immediately on arrival in the U.S. from Cuidad Trujillo, which happened even before the announcement was made of the actual purchase of his contract by Brooklyn... The same day, Dan Bankhead dropped his luggage in the room with Don Newcombe, his new teammate in Montreal... One of Bankhead's greatest boosters, incidentally, is Jackie Robinson, whom many thought cared little for the pitcher... "If he gets the work he needs in the International League, he'll be back next year as one of the best pitchers in baseball," predicts Robbie.

The Bums' chartered DC-4 set down here in Fort Worth at 6:15 P.M. Friday, exactly six hours and five minutes after departure from Vero Beach... Jackie Robinson, who seems to suffer a chronic stomach disturbance, had a rough time and was glad to get down... Robinson, Campanella and two colored newsmen were housed at a private home at 924 Irma St. The white members of the party, players and press stayed at the Texas Hotel... Campanella's first move was to put in a long-distance call to his wife, Ruthie, in New York... Robinson elected to wait one day to give his wife, Rachel, who left Los Angeles by car Tuesday, ample time to reach Gotham... She'll stop at the Hotel McAlpin and await Jackie's arrival, April 12.

The casual manner in which Fort Worth players received Jackie Robinson and Roy Campanella is noteworthy. There was no sign of disagreement whatsoever, and several went out of their way to strike up conversations... This was particularly true of Outfielder Irv Noren who played basketball with Jackie in Los Angeles in the winter of 1946-47... Manager Les Burge may or may not have something to do with this. Burge was a first baseman when Robbie covered second for the pennant-winning Montreal Royals in 1946.

The "colored" stands were two-thirds full at 1:30 P.M. Saturday for a 3:15 P.M. game, and were completely occupied by 1 P.M. Sunday for a game at the same time... Robinson spent a large part of Sunday's pregame hours conversing with white patrons in the field boxes... Among these patrons was an unidentified big-hatted Texan who devoted much time Saturday to heckling the Dodger first baseman about his racial connection. Jackie talked at length with him Sunday and left him smiling... Jackie was held up for nearly 20 minutes after Saturday's tilt, signing autographs for white kids who stormed the Dodger dugout and prevented his leaving.

August 28, 1948

When Satchel Paige finished dusting off the Chicago White Sox with three hits for his fifth win Friday at Cleveland, someone said, "Satch, it looks like you're the rookie of the year," to which the Lean One drawled, "You may be right man, but 22 years sure is a long time to be a rookie."

He was alluding, of course, to the length of time he spent in colored baseball... I got to thinking what a sad commentary it would be on major league baseball if Satchel were to come up as the 1948 Rookie of the Year at 44 years of age.

Looking up at the record crowd of 78,382 admissions, the outspoken "rookie" observed: "Gee man, I oughta be working on a percentage of the gate. It wasn't nothing like this at Kansas City. . . I just threw fast balls up there [at the White Sox]," Paige told *The Afro*. . . "When a pitch is working, I just keep using it. . . Didn't curve one till the eighth, then I got a strikeout."

Jim Hegan, Tribe catcher, agreed with Satchel that the long pitcher was "faster than he has been" since joining the Indians. . . "Yeah," said Hegan, "I guess Satch was 'quicker' than I've seem him. He's easy to hold too. All his pitches are in or real near the strike zone."

Satchel Paige says he has all kinds of pitches, some of which "I ain't even showed yet." He says he calls 'em "bloopers, loopers and droopers. . . I got a jump ball, a screw ball, a be ball, a wobbly ball, a whipsy-dipsy, a nothin' ball and a bat dodger.". . . The Lean One admits he has remarkable control. Like the shrinking violet he is, he says: "It ain't my fault I got control, I was born with it." Of his hesitation pitch, he says: "Some of the umpires have been saying they're going to call a balk on me if I throw my 'hesitation' with a man on third. I guess if they do, that'll just have to be all right. But it won't be no balk. The rules say a balk is a pitch that fools a base runner. If I wind up, the base runner knows I can't throw to catch him so I got to throw home. So when I wind up with my 'hesitation,' I ain't fooling the runner, I'm fooling the batter. Ain't that what a pitcher's supposed to do?"

April 2, 1949

VERO BEACH, FLA.—A white cop walks over to your reporter during Sunday's game, a few minutes after Jackie Robinson was removed on account of injury. . . "Looka here," he says, "Why don't you put in the paper about them Brooklyn Dodgers?. . . You oughta tell 'em about taking Robinson out with all them people here. . . A lot of 'em come from Fort Pierce and Palm Beach, and some of 'em come from Jacksonville, more than 200 miles from here. . . They oughta either let 'em play or release him. . . These people want to see him. . . *That's what they got him for anyway.*"

ORLANDO, FLA.—My father would have loved this day. . . The Old Man died last spring, still a loyal rooter for the Washington Senators, but adamant in his refusal to attend any of the games at Griffith Stadium in Washington as his own personal protest against President Clark Griffith's attitude toward colored baseball players. . . Pop had been a die-hard for the Senators and hadn't missed a game in the 20 years previous to 1947. . . Knew Walter Johnson, Clyde Milan, Joe Judge, Sam Rice, Bucky Harris and many others . . . they called him by name. . . One of his keepsakes was a letter from Griffith inviting him to the Walter Johnson Day celebration, in which the Senators' president addressed him, "Dear Sam," and signed himself "Clark"... But just before the opening of the 1947 season, Pop wrote Griffith and told him he was sorry, but he felt he wouldn't wish to attend any more Washington games, "because of your expressed opposition to integration, not only on your own club, but in the whole of organized baseball"... Griffith's reply regretted the action, and said, "It is sincere hope that someday, you will experience a change of heart"... Last week, it was Clark Griffith admitting "a change of heart" and telling the Old Man's son that he is "on the lookout for a good, young colored player" for his Senators.

WEST PALM BEACH, FLA.—Colored fandom gave such heavy support to the Philadelphia Athletics' spring training gate for the Brooklyn Dodger games that Connie Mack (who can't see colored players on his team) pulled one of the oldest tricks known to the "hustling" fraternity... For the first game, the "colored" admission was 75 cents... But, when these same patrons arrived at the park for the second contest, they were confronted by signs setting the price of ducats at $1.20, a 45-cent hike on the "suckers"... Incidentally, when the Athletics and Washington Senators played their lily-white games the day prior to the Dodgers-A's tilt, a paid "crowd" of 619 was on hand.

When Manager Burt Shotton switched from his plan to let Bruce Edwards catch last Sunday's game here, and placed Roy Campanella behind the bat, it was because Connie Mack had asked him to do so... Yet, Campanella, who was born, raised and educated in Philadelphia, a few blocks from Shibe Park, isn't wanted on Mack's team... He "worked out" under the eyes of Phillies' officials in 1946, and heard nothing more from it... This is the second of nine cities destined to get their first glimpse of tan players in organized baseball via the Dodgers' spring training junket... Others in the order in which they appear on the schedule are Beaumont, San Antonio and Houston, Texas; Macon and Atlanta, Georgia; Greenville, South Carolina and Charlotte, North Carolina.

HAINES CITY, FLA.—This town's colored fans are being admitted to spring training exhibition games for the first time in history... In previous years when the Baltimore Orioles—and before them, the Kansas City Blues—trained here, only white fans were admitted to the park... When they turned out for the first games played by the Newark Bears, Yale Field workmen had to hurriedly construct a makeshift "colored" stand... This reporter, looking for the "colored restroom," was directed to a tree about 35 yards off from where the rightfield foul line ended.

Luis Marquez, the former Homestead Grays' outfielder, appears to be set for the Newark Bears' centerfield post, despite the "grandstanding" tendency for which he is noted among tan league stars... Gene Collins has a 50-50 chance of sticking, depending on the kind of pitching help the Bears get from the parent New York Yankees... Frank Austin is extremely doubtful... Lew Riggs, white third base veteran who played with Jackie Robinson, when the latter was initiated at Montreal, is a player-coach on the Newark roster... Buddy Hassett, manager of the Bears, says he frequently played against Satchel Paige, Josh Gibson, Jim Beckwith, Dick Lundy, Martin Dihigo and other such stars of 15 years ago... He rates the late Josh and Beckwith as "two of the best hitters baseball has ever known."

VERO BEACH, FLA.—Sammy Jethroe is rapidly gaining the reputation of being the Dodgertown Satchel Paige... His quick wit and dry humor are traits of the likes of Paige and Joe Louis... The other day, Al Campanis, an instructor here, asked Jethroe: "Do you think you could run faster if you wore track shoes and trunks?"... Sammy, who had just set a record for the 60-yard Dodgertown cinder track, replied: "Why, of course. I could run faster in these things I have on (baseball spikes and uniform) if I wanted to... Shucks! I just run fast enough now to beat these other fellows. I ain't racing no time clocks... I'm a ballplayer, I ain't no track man"... Jocko Conlan, the colorful National League umpire who is here working the Dodgers' spring exhibition games, says he played against "a number of the old-time colored ballplayers"... "And you can believe me," says Conlan, "there were always some really great players, especially fellows like Rube Foster and Binga DeMoss."

Dan Bankhead arrived in camp Tuesday and joined his St. Paul teammates... He had to leave wife, Linda, in Puerto Rico, where she is expecting a visit from Sir Stork momentarily... Jackie Robinson is showing mild concern over the approaching visit to Atlanta and Macon, Georgia, next month... "I'm still going," declared Jackie the other day. "I have no other thought... I only hope the folks who don't want Campy and me won't make it unpleasant for our teammates"... Roy Campanella has been signed to a contract endorsing a popular cigarette.

April 9, 1949

VERO BEACH, FLA.—It is now just past 3 P.M. Tuesday and the Brooklyn Dodgers' westbound DC-4 has been in the air almost four hours... I'm using the dateline of our taking off point because there's no way of knowing just where we are... Looking out the window, there is nothing to see, but rolls upon rolls of angry-looking clouds... Obviously, a disturbance of some kind is raging beneath us... The big ship has been batted like a tennis ball the past 40 or 50 minutes... It's ticklish stuff.

Sudden dips and vigorous twists have done queer things to the plane... No one has said as much, but on the faces of most of the passengers has been a look of grave concern, as though there is a general expectancy that the next jerk or twist is going to snap us in half like one does a dry twig a mid-autumn... That look, though, is not on the faces of the big, strong, virile guys like Jackie Robinson, Ralph Branca, Rex Barney, Gil Hodges and Coach Jake Pitler... Each has involuntarily donned a sickly mask and there isn't one among them who can still claim ownership of anything he has eaten since the day before yesterday... Now, they tell us where we are... We're over Beaumont, Texas, our destination... We have been for 30 minutes, but because the ceiling over the field is only 200 feet and our big ship needs not less than 400 feet, we can't land... 30 minutes and 78 miles later, we're set down in Houston.

BEAUMONT, TEX.—The usual "Jim Crow twist" was given reverse English Wednesday when Brooklyn visited here for the first game of the spring exhibition tour... Instead of barring the Dodgers' colored players from the clubhouse, Stuart Stadium officials "suggested" that Jackie Robinson and Roy Campanella use the players' quarters at the park and the rest of the team dress at their hotel... It so happened that the unfinished dressing room floor was covered with mud and water, shower facilities were incomplete and the place was entirely devoid of window covering.

Undoubtedly, this the most backward town from a race relations' standpoint, the Dodgers have played in their two years of spring barnstorming... Booing, filthy name-calling and insults of varied and sundry degrees have greeted each appearance of Robinson and Campanella on the field and at the plate... In the press coop, the public address man, known as "Tiny," identifies the two ballplayers only as "the n--s"... The official scorer spends more time picking out one patron after another in the colored section for ridicule, than he puts into watching the game.

Jackie, Campy and I arrived here at 10:35 A.M., after a two-hour train ride from Houston, where we spent last night... We went straight to the ballpark, where we were met by a line two blocks long and four, five and six deep, already standing before the colored ticket booths... Park officials agreed that they had seen nothing like it before... Although the weather was "neither fit for man nor beast," faithfuls fought like mad to cling to their advance positions in the line ... and late-comers who overran the field, braved ankle-deep mud for nine innings of uninteresting ball ... and after the game, hundreds stood vigil in a driving rain outside the dressing room, awaiting the Robinson-Campanella autographs... Incidentally, the colored players dressed at the clubhouse here, the others donned their uniforms at their hotel.

SAN ANTONIO, TEX.—Arriving here shortly after midnight Thursday in two special cars, the Dodgers slept until 8:30 A.M., after which the white players and the newsmen repaired to the downtown Gunter Hotel... We have been cared for very nicely by Valmo Bellinger, a local bigwig, and his brother, Harry... On the train, as is always the case with the Dodger organization, we are all a part of one baseball family... For instance, Cal Abrams occupied the berth over me, Dee Fondy slept over Campy and Clarence Podbielan was Jackie's section mate.

An interesting thing happened today, a sequel to an occurrence yesterday at Beaumont... Robbie, conscious of the tremendous partisanship in the stands at Beaumont told teammates: "I'm going to try my best in batting practice to hit one out of the park and watch the colored stands go wild... Then, I'm going to swing like hell on the next pitch and miss... I want to see what the white's reaction will be"... He did just that... When his first hit bounced of the fence, the colored patrons broke into a wild demonstration... When he whiffed on the next pitch, the white section became a bedlam of hoots and catcalls... Today, during the game, the typical Dixie attitude prevailed again, and the closeness of the Bums, one to the other, was revealed... Jackie stole second in the fourth and there was unrestricted whooping in one section of the park... A moment later, he was thrown out trying to reach third on a fly to right, and happiness reigned supreme in the other part... Pee Wee Reese, a Southern boy from Kentucky, spoke up: "We can all home now. *Everybody's* happy!"

April 23, 1949

"Indians' Tan Trio Compelled to Walk to Ballpark by Bigoted Texas Taxis"

TEXARKANA, TEX.—This is a small town in the hinterlands of deepest Texas. And, in keeping with practice in Texas, white taxicabs refuse to haul colored passengers—although it is frequently done in Dallas, Fort Worth and San Antonio.

Anyway, last week when the Cleveland Indians were in town with their three colored stars, Larry Doby, Satchel Paige and Orestes Minoso, the taxicabs refused to haul them to the ballpark. Since there were no colored cabs available, and since the Indians were expecting them to play in the game against the New York Giants that afternoon, the three players set out to walk.

It was a distance of 1.5 miles from their hotel to the ballpark and Doby, Paige and Minoso walked it. Also, since they were advised that they would not be able to use the clubhouse at the park, the trio walked it in their uniforms.

They arrived more than 30 minutes late, but they arrived. Doby was obviously peeved. Paige, an old trooper, who lets nothing ruffle him, appeared unmoved. Minoso, carefree in the mold of the average Cuban, laughed about it.

The latter was so unperturbed that he slammed a two-run homer to thrill the taxi drivers who passed him up on their way to see the game.

April 1, 1950

"Campy, Jackie as Dodgers: Integration in Dixie Halts When Players Leave Field"

VERO BEACH, FLA.—If the reports emanating from this quarter are so glowing as to give the impression everything in baseball's integration experiment is now honey and whipped cream, let me assure you that is far from the truth.

The blame for such a misconception—if one be alive—perhaps rests with me. It is very probably due to the rose-colored glasses I so frequently don when this type of assignment comes my way.

Regardless of any impressions you may have gotten to the contrary, the South has not accepted inter-racialism in baseball. It is merely tolerating it.

Jackie Robinson, Roy Campanella, Don Newcombe and Dan Bankhead are recognized in Dixie as Brooklyn Dodger baseball players, sure. But they are also recognized as colored men.

SOUTH STILL THE "SOUTH"

And to "Mr. and Mrs. Southerner," the latter fact takes precedence over the former. The monkey-suits of Ebbets Field don't give them first-class citizenship any more than do their gray or blue civilian clothes and brown faces.

To them, and to me, the South is still the South.

Once we leave Dodgertown, the city within the city of Vero Beach, Fla., we are on our own. White members of the organization go in one direction; we cross the railroad tracks and go the other way.

Whenever and wherever possible, Dixie whites waste no time reminding us what has been the status quo for more than 84 years.

SOME IMPROVEMENT NOTED

In fairness however, it should be pointed out here that there are some white southerners whose attitudes have improved considerably. These greatly outnumbered few have disclosed a friendship that is gratifying.

But for the most part, the traditional animosity prevails. Not always vocal, but always present.

Two weeks ago, three of the players—Robinson, Campy and Newcombe—as well as your reporter, used a car for the trip to Miami for the game with the Boston Braves. The machine was a rental obtained by the Dodgers' road secretary, Harold Parrott, from a Vero Beach drive-yourself company, for his own use around the base.

CAR RENTAL BIAS

In order to circumvent any likely embarrassment evolving from roadside eating, etc., we were given use of the car for transportation to and from Miami, and, once we were in town, to and from the ballpark.

Somehow, the car rental company learned we had used the machine, and the next day, Parrott was requested to return it immediately. Officials of the agency made no effort to conceal the reason for its sudden decision. "No niggers" can drive their cars, they fumed.

A few days later, Campanella was named as the lone colored player on a squad to play in West Palm Beach. En route back to Vero Beach, the team stopped for dinner at a roadside inn.

FORCED TO EAT IN BUS

Several players who are on the squad for no more than tryouts and who will end up in Class A or B ball, went in, sat at the tables and ordered what they wished. Campanella, generally recognized as the best catcher in baseball, was forced to sit alone in the bus and eat what was brought out to him on a tray.

Again, a few days later, Campy bore the brunt of responsibility of showing at least one colored player in a game at West Palm Beach. This time, to play it safe, he ate dinner in West Palm Beach and then took a late train to Vero Beach.

When he arrived at 2 A.M., he discovered that there had been a mix-up of instructions at the base and there was no one on hand to meet him.

White taxicabs refused to take him as a fare, and the result was the star catcher has to walk the estimated 2.5 miles to the base.

The southern treatment has played no favorites, Each of us, at one time or another, has been confronted with indignities and inconveniences that Dixie reactionaries seem to save especially for colored persons.

REPORTER STOPPED TWICE

The other day, en route to Vero Beach, your reporter had a small case of the poison administered. Twice in the five-mile round-trip, I was stopped by city cops and made to show my operator's license and car credentials for no apparent reason other than I was a colored man driving a Lincoln Cosmopolitan (belonging to Dan Bankhead).

Perhaps, I should make it clear that it isn't only during the Spring that the Brown Bums meet up with this sort of thing.

It happens in the regular season too.

Dodger brass was forced to change its Philadelphia hotel because the management frowned at the thought of housing colored ballplayers with the whites. Since 1948, the Brooks have been lodging at the Warwick.

ROOM SERVICE ONLY

In Cincinnati, while the Netherlands-Plaza accepts the whole group, it is "suggested" that the colored members of the party stay out of the dining room. A special arrangement is made whereby their meals are served in their rooms.

The Dodgers' hotel in St. Louis is the Chase. On arrival in that city, the white players take cabs in one direction and the colored in another.

Last September when the Brooks went into St. Louis for their final crucial series with the Cardinals, the party split up as usual.

POOR ACCOMMODATIONS

Inferior ballplayers, some just up from the minors as low as Class B, packed away to exquisite Chase. Many of them couldn't carry Jackie's bat or Campanella's glove or Newk's rosin bag. But, they went to their first class accommodation.

The four of us squeezed into a third-class hotel in the colored section, Jackie and Campy having to put up together. Newcombe, who was slated to pitch the next day, spent the night trying to sleep in a room located directly over a constantly screeching jukebox. I fitted myself into a basement room the size of an overfed telephone booth.

For an inconsequential sportswriter, that was a pardonable sin. But, think what irony Southern prejudice was dealing put in the case of the others.

ONLY COLOR COUNTED

While Class B squirts were lounging in luxury at the town's best hostelry, Robbie, the National League's Most Valuable Player; Newcombe, the 1949 Rookie of the Year; and Campy, the greatest catcher in the game, were trying to find rest in a Jim Crow house in what many cities in Dixie call "Colored Town."

Uptown, in air-conditioned splendor, were three players on whom the Dodgers had asked waivers, meaning they could be had by any other club that wanted them for $10,000 each.

Downtown, in heat and noise and all-round discomfort, were three players whose combined value could conservatively be estimated at $1 million.

June 17, 1950

I dare say the movie folk and even Jackie Robinson himself, aren't going to like me for saying this, but following the dictates of an honest reporter, I'm forced to say *The Jackie Robinson Story* isn't... It isn't because it isn't the true story... If anything was ever "Hollywooded" to death, this most certainly was ... my reason for making such a charge is as plain and unemotional as a hot dog... Jackie's life story, done accurately, would have been every bit as moving and exciting as a motion picture could possibly hope for... This version is full of fictitious sequences, all uncalled for ... and worst of all, it is dishonest... Hollywood literally "broke its back" trying to prove the white players on both the Montreal and Brooklyn clubs were openly hostile to Jackie his first two years in the organization ... the film even has one player on an opposing team straddling Jackie while he is on the ground from a slide into second, and pummeling him about the head and body ... nothing could be further from the truth... There has been no instance in Jackie's four years in organized ball, where any player has so much as taken a swing at him... I was with Robinson in the spring of 1946 and again in the spring of 1947 ... it was obvious that several of his teammates were lacking in warmth for Robbie, but there was never the open hostility of which the film makes capital.

Omitted for some reason — probably because of the pressure of time — were legitimate shots, which, quite plausibly, could have been worked into the flicker ... like having to live in the third-class Los Angeles Hotel in Havana while his white teammates were being put up at the Academia Militaire during spring training in 1947 ... like having to search from one end of the Cuban capital to the other, hoping to find a decent place to eat

... and like being forced to ride taxi 22 miles each day to and from his hotel to the training grounds... These things and countless others might well have been included, while the hitherto untold conversation between Branch Rickey and Clay Hopper was left out... Hopper, a Mississippian, could surprise nobody by asking if Rickey actually considered Jackie "a human being" ... but, Hopper after learning more about colored athletes—proved himself to be high-water okay ... an excellent self-disciplinarian, Hopper conquered his prejudices and since doing so, he has been a real friend to Jackie and each of the other three tan players now with the Dodgers.

All along the line leading up to showing of the film, baseball writers traveling with the Dodgers were told this was to be a wholesome, authentic baseball picture... Yet, the few acted baseball scenes that were kept in the movie are as unreal and unconvincing as a Mickey Mouse comic... Jackie, admittedly, is not an actor, he's a ballplayer... But in the film, he acts better than he plays ... the way he fields and the manner in which he goes down to avoid "dust off" pitches would make on think that Jackie had never gotten in or out of the way of a ball in his life ... to those of us who know Robinson as a nimble guy so light on his feet that he could skate on a feather, the clumsy, bulbous figure of the movie is hardly recognizable.

WENDELL SMITH

The Best of His Generation

Who was the best black sportswriter of his generation? To Sam Lacy of *The Baltimore Afro-American,* it was his colleague, the late Wendell Smith.

"Anybody can be a reporter—a kid coming home from school and telling his parents what happened in class that day is a reporter—but it takes more to be a journalist," said Lacy, himself an accomplished scribe. "Wendell had that something extra. He was always thinking ahead and never quite satisfied with what he had accomplished."

Smith spent just over a decade at *The Pittsburgh Courier,* arriving there shortly after graduating from West Virginia State College in 1937. Almost immediately, his substantial, topical and occasionally whimsical style blossomed.

"Unconfirmed report: Satchel Paige is pitching for the Atlanta Black Crackers these fine spring days . . . and it is not down in South America," Smith wrote in a 1938 short. "Run Satch! The cops up this way have been looking all over for you! Personal message to the mighty Satchel: When you refused to sign with the Pittsburgh Crawfords and suddenly disappeared, it is reported that your wife, Janet, tried to influence a number of the other players to quit the team and follow you. When [Crawfords owner] Gus Greenlee found out her intentions, he fired her as a waitress in his Crawford Grill.

"Thirty thousand spectators at the recent East-West game in Chicago proves that Negro baseball has something. Negro moguls are going to keep fooling around until some white folks step in and take the game away from them, making thousands of dollars off the same teams that are losing money now."

Smith covered Negro league baseball like a blanket. His style could be folksy, but it turned direct when he was taking on both major league and black team owners. In addition to writing some of the very first interviews and player profiles of personalities in Pittsburgh's colorful baseball

Wendell Smith (photo courtesy The Chicago Defender*).*

scene, he also fit the aggressive, sometimes angry style of *Courier* Editor Robert L. Vann, who launched the paper on numerous crusades to benefit black America. One of those crusades, a 1939 drive to integrate the major leagues, centered on a series of lengthy, exhaustive pieces written primarily by Smith.

"[Smith] had a vision of an American society, where ability, skill and character are the sole measures of a man and not the color of his skin," wrote *The Chicago Defender* after his death in 1972. "He pursued that idealism ... not with the militancy of the new breed of black spokesman, rather with the calm and patient logic of a wise man whose vision was sharp enough to see the light at the end of the tunnel. He has made his contribution. History will not pass him by."

Jules Tygiel in *Baseball's Great Experiment* calls Smith "the most talented and influential of the black journalists" of the era. "He could be bitterly sarcastic and vitriolic in his rage against Jim Crow," Tygiel writes, "yet lyrical in his descriptive prose."

As the ghostwriter of *Jackie Robinson—My Own Story,* published in 1948, Smith is the reporter most closely identified with Robinson. Smith and Sam Lacy accompanied Robinson and the Dodgers in 1947, the year the major league color ban was finally broken, and the three men became close friends, Lacy recalls. Indeed, Robinson himself once said he would never have made it to the big leagues without Smith's help.

One telling story of Smith's drive to integrate the major leagues came in the spring of 1945, when he had just returned from Boston where token tryouts had been held by the Boston Red Sox for three Negro league players—Robinson, Sam Jethroe and Marvin Williams. As Smith sat through a post-workout press conference, Dodgers' general manager Branch Rickey motioned him aside to ask if he knew of any blacks talented enough to play in the big leagues. "If you aren't serious about this, Mr. Rickey," he replied, "I'd rather not waste our time discussing it. But if you are serious, I do know of a player who could make it. His name is Jackie Robinson."

Smith grew up in Detroit, where his father was Henry Ford's chef. An accomplished athlete as a young man, Smith pitched for an integrated Detroit American Legion team, but found his path to the major leagues blocked by the color ban. In 1933, after he pitched his team to a 1–0 victory in a playoff game, a scout signed both his catcher Mike Tresh and the game's losing pitcher to contracts. The scout told Smith that he wanted to sign him as well, but couldn't. Smith later used that incident as an inspiration for his decision to become a sportswriter and work for baseball integration.

Like most other black sportswriters of his generation, Smith worked his baseball coverage into the crowded demands of the newspaper beat. He joined *The Courier* in 1937, and within a year was the paper's assistant sports editor, columnist and city editor. By 1940, Chester Washington moved to the city editor's desk, and Smith became sports editor, serving there until he left the paper for Chicago in 1947.

Smith also covered boxing, and he was considered one of the country's top boxing experts, writing extensively about Joe Louis, Ezzard Charles and Rocky Marciano. In addition to the Robinson book, he ghostwrote books by Roy Campanella, Joe Louis and Ernie Banks, and was also among the first crop of black beat writers to cover the Olympics—the 1948 summer games in London.

From *The Courier,* Smith moved to *Chicago Today,* later called *The Chicago American,* where he covered the major leagues. In 1963, Smith moved to television, as sports editor for WBBM-TV, and the following year, joined WGN-TV's "People to People" Sunday program. He also kept to the newspaper beat, writing a weekly sports column for *The Chicago Sun-Times.*

Along the way, Smith became a decorated member of the Negro league beat writers. He received the 1951 "Alumnus of the Year" at West Virginia State College, the Hearst Organization's top sportswriting award in 1958, the Chicago Press Club's "Best Sportswriter" award for 1959, and just this year because the first black member of the Writers' Wing of the Baseball Hall of Fame. When he died at 58 from cancer, Smith was president of the Chicago Press Club.

Ironically, Smith died in November 1972, just one month and two days after Jackie Robinson's death. After all, wrote *The Defender,* "Smith's judgment that black players were ready for the major leagues was justified by Robinson's stellar performance in baseball, followed by other black players who are giving a good account of themselves, not only in baseball but also in all other sports."

The stories that follow were written for *The Pittsburgh Courier.*

May 11, 1938

"A Strange Tribe"

Why we continue to flock to major league ball parks, spending our hard earned dough, screaming and hollering, stamping our feet and clapping our hands, begging and pleading for some white batter to knock some white pitcher's ears off, almost having fits if the home team loses and crying for joy when they win, is a question that probably never will be answered satisfactorily. What in the world are we thinking about anyway?

NOT WANTED

The fact that major league baseball refuses to admit Negro players within its folds makes the question just that much more perplexing. Surely, it's sufficient reason for us to quit spending our money and time in their ball parks. Major league baseball does not want us. It never has. Still, we continue to help support this institution that places a bold "Not Welcome" sign over its thriving portal and refuse to patronize the very place that has shown that it is more than welcome to have us. We black folks are a strange tribe!

MAKING PROGRESS

Negro baseball is still in its infancy. In the last 10 years, it has come a long, long way. Gone are the days when the players having the most knives and razors won the ball game. Gone are the days when the teams appeared before the public dressed like scarecrows and reminded us of the lost legion. Gone are the days when only one or two good players were on a team. Now, their rosters are filled with brilliant, colorful, dazzling players who know the game from top to bottom. Negro teams now have everything the white clubs have. Except of course, the million dollar ball parks to play in, parks that we helped to build with our hard earned dollars. Nevertheless, we ignore them and go to see teams play that do not give a hang whether we come or not.

Sounds silly, doesn't it? Well—it's true! Despite the fact that we have our own teams and brilliant players, the most colorful in the world, mind you we go elsewhere and get a kick out of doing it. Suckers! You said it brother!

NO ENCOURAGEMENT

They're real troopers, these guys who risk their money and devote their lives to Negro baseball. We black folk offer no encouragement and don't seem to care of they make a go of it or not. We literally ignore them completely. With our noses high and our hands deep in our pockets, squeezing the same dollar that we hand out to the white players, we walk past their ball parks and go the major league game. Nuts—that's what we are. Just plain nuts!

FROM DIXIE

Listen! if any one of us wanted to talk to one of the ballplayers whom we've been spending our hard earned dough on, screaming and hollering, stamping our feet and clapping our hands for, we'd probably be ignored. If he did speak to us, it would probably be a disrespectful salutation. Such as "Hello George," or "What ya' say Sam." Or maybe even worse than that. Oh, he wouldn't eh! That's what you think. Don't forget that he comes from Mississippi, Georgia, Texas or any other place you can think of below the Mason-Dixon Line. And he's white! He looks upon us as something the cat brought in. Even though he is playing ball in a northern city, making northern money, he still looks upon us that way. He's a leopard and you know what they say about their spots. You can't change 'em.

TOUGH FIGHT

We have been fighting for years in an effort to make owners of major league baseball teams admit Negro players. But they won't do it, probably never will. We keep on crawling, begging and pleading for recognition just the same. We know that they don't want us, but we still keep giving them our money. Keep on going to their ball games and shouting till we are blue in the face. Oh, we're an optimistic, faithful, prideless lot—we pitiful black folk.

Yes sir—we black folk are a strange tribe!

June 11, 1938

"The New Gas House Gang"

If there is any team in Negro baseball that comes near approaching the "Gas House Gang" category, it is the Homestead Grays, who are already well out in front of rival teams in the National League, and from all indications bound to cop their second pennant in a row.

The St. Louis Cardinals of the major leagues gained considerable fame when they had brothers Dizzy and Daffy Dean throwing their fast balls at the opposition, and Pepper Martin was raising havoc with everything opposing pitchers tossed up to the plate, besides running wild on the bases. Known as the "Gas House Gang," the Cardinals played rough and tumble baseball, fought among themselves nearly every day of the week, and never gave an opposing team anything that was unnecessary. This year, however, the "Gas House Gang" miss the services of brothers Dizzy and Daffy Dean. It is just another ball club.

TOUGH BOYS

The "Gas House Gang" of Negro baseball are the same type of rough and tumble bunch that the Cardinals were in their heyday. They play the game for all they can get out of it. Every ball game is played as though it meant the difference between life and death. They ask for nothing, and give nothing in return. The Homestead Grays might be called the new "Gas House Gang."

Josh Gibson, Buck Leonard and Ray Brown are the leaders of this new "Gas House Gang." Gibson, Leonard and Brown are not only young, but they give that certain something known as "spark." They are the spark plugs that keep the Grays on top of the heap. Any of the three can do the things that a leader of a "Gas House Gang" must do—hit, run, throw and fight, the last of which is the most important. Along with Carlisle, Benjamin, Jackson and Manager Vic Harris, Gibson, Leonard and Brown are the nucleus of what might be the greatest team in Negro baseball of all time within the next two years.

Not only are the Grays champions of Negro baseball, but they are a cocky bunch of ballplayers. They do not believe that any team can beat them. They don't give a hoot for umpires, fans, newspapermen, or anything else. Baseball is all they care about—it is their life.

COCKY BUNCH

You can ask any of the Grays who they think will cop the pennant this year, and before you finish your sentence, the player will say: "Why, we're going to win it again. Who did you think? We've got the best team in baseball and of anyone doubts it, all they have to do is come play against us." Or at least words to that effect.

The Grays have the best defensive ball club in baseball. The only weak spot in the whole team is at third base, where Jack Johnson, a rookie, is playing. Johnson is expected to fill the gap at the hot corner and so far has been doing a fairly good job. However, he cannot be compared yet with Jackson at short, Carlisle at second, or Leonard at first. They are three of the best infielders in the country, and would shine on any major league club when it comes to picking and scooping up hot grounders. In the outfield, Harris, Benjamin and Williams comprise a great trio of fly chasers. Ray Brown, Walker, Duke Wiemaker and Partlow make it the Gas House Gang's firing line.

TAKING IT EASY

The Grays have had an easy time of it so far this year. As yet, they have never been pushed by a league team in a series. They have walloped every team they've met and will probably be doing it all year. Now that Leon Day, Newark's ace hurler, is on the bench due to a sore back, it's difficult to see how any team will stop the Gas Housers.

They're an ungrateful, conceited, devil-may-care group of ballplayers, these Homesteaders. They know that there is nothing that they cannot beat on a ball diamond. The New York Yankees or Giants are just two other ball clubs to them, and they feel not one bit inferior to these mighty teams of the majors. They pack power, punch, fight and cockiness . . . this new edition of the Gas House Gang!

When the Grays will fall from the pinnacle of Negro baseball is impossible to forecast right now. They outclass the other clubs to such a degree that it would be better for the league if the team was split up and the men sent away to other teams. But, of course, that will never happen.

July 23, 1938

"With the '.400'"

We have always wanted to mingle with individuals who are classified within that most exclusive circle known as the "Four Hundred." Although we have never had a burning desire to "join up" with that contingent of selected personalities, it has always been a yen of ours to see just what makes them tick. We've always been interested, more or less, in the other half.

That's why we recently took time out to have a chat with Walter Fenner "Buck" Leonard. During the winter months, Mr. Leonard resides in the tranquil little town of Rocky Mount, North Carolina. In the summer, he spends his valuable time socking singles, doubles, triples and home runs for the Homestead Grays, from the jagged, rocky-bound coast of Maine to the sunny shores of California.

HITTING .480

Mr. Walter "Buck" Leonard is currently blasting that horsehide seam stitched pellet for an average of .480. Which makes him 80 points better than the ".400." And when a guy is 80 points above the ".400," he deserves to be given the once over. Anybody pretending to be a baseball fan knows that when a man is hitting .300 or better, he's doing a right smart job. But when he hits .400 or better, he's sticking his nose right into the door that leads to the Hall of Fame.

BEST IN LOOP

Buck Leonard is without a doubt the best first baseman in Negro baseball. And until last week, when he got his left thumb, his bat and a burning fast ball all mixed up at the same time in a game in Baltimore, Maryland, he has been playing the most sensational ball of his brilliant career. Only once this year has he failed to get a base hit in a league contest, and his great fielding is one of the main reasons why the Grays are breezing along at the top of the Negro National League. Last year, Buck finished the season with an average of .383, and had hammered out 36 home runs before the curtain fell.

Buck takes his baseball seriously. Just like the other players on the Grays, he goes out to win every game, regardless of who or where it is being played. He's the kind of guy you like as soon as you meet him. Quiet and unimpressed over his brilliant record, this Carolina clubber loves to play baseball. It's his second love. Sara Sorrell Leonard is his first love. She is his wife.

MARRIED LAST YEAR

Sara and Buck "signed up" on December 30, last year. While he is laying Negro National League pitchers low during the summer, Sara is doing a like job down in Rocky Mount as a mortician. When Buck goes home in the fall, Sara will again take up her school teaching duties, and he will continue to study for his license as a certified mortician.

Buck doesn't intend to end up like most ballplayers. He hopes to have a fine business built up by the time his playing days are over, and live quietly down in Rocky Mount as a mortician. When he finally does quit playing, it's almost a sure bet that opposing pitchers will gladly give him a farewell party. However, he's only 30 years old, and from all indications, they will have to wait quite awhile. In the meantime, he'll be around blasting their ears off.

NOT SNOOTY

Even though he's a member of the ".400," we found out that there is nothing snooty about him. Everywhere he goes, he has a host of admirers and well-wishers. When he smiles, which is most of the time, he displays a set of teeth that would take a dentist's breath. That's how near perfect they are. He has played ball in 44 of the 48 states and in three foreign countries. But, as he puts it, "There's no place like Rocky Mount."

Buck Leonard is a perfect example of the modern day Negro athlete. Like [Joe] Louis and Louis Armstrong, [Jesse] Owens and all the rest, he's one swell guy.

August 24, 1940

Big Josh Gibson had returned from far away Venezuela, where he spent the past three-and-one-half months plastering out home runs for the enthusiastic natives, and by virtue of his mighty wallops, his name has become a household word down there.

He played down in Caracas and did all right for himself. He played in 10 games, hit four home runs and smacked the horsehide for a .347 average. Most important of all, he got paid on the 1st and the 15th of the month. And for playing in one game a week, sometimes two, Josh hauled down $600 per month, which ain't peanuts when you come to think of it.

"The owners here in the States get angry with us," Josh said, "when we go away. But what would you do if a company offered you twice as much money for doing just half as much work."

I told him just what I'd do.

"Well, that's what we did," he said. "We went down there and played ball once or twice a week and loafed the rest of the time. They paid me twice as much salary, my room and board and transportation expenses down there. They did the same for the rest of the American players they brought down there."

The big catcher whom Walter Johnson, ex-major league star, said was as good a catcher as the Yanks' Bill Dickey and worth $200,000 to any big league team, is in the pink of condition and anxious to get back in the harness here. He said he will join the Homestead Grays and play in exhibition games. He is barred from the Negro National League because the moguls turned thumbs down on the players who quit the ranks for foreign soil.

The rule the league adopted against players jumping to foreign countries has always seemed rather absurd to this corner because it has no more meaning than a Munich Pact or Treaty. In the first place, it is designed to prevent a player from going where he can get more bread and butter than he can here. In Puerto Rico and Venezuela, they haul down twice as much cash. No owner in the States can pay Josh Gibson, Bill Perkins, Harry Williams or any other top-notch star the pay in those countries.

It sounds a bit communistic trying to prevent a player from going where he can better himself financially, and as a result, have enough shackles left over for a rainy day. But that's precisely what the owners of the teams in the Negro National League have been trying to do.

The moguls are justified in forcing players to live up to the contracts here in the States. But a player who decides it is to his advantage to leave the country and travel 1,600 miles to make more money certainly should not be censored. Nobody in his right mind is going 1,600 miles to play baseball or anything else unless it is decidedly to their advantage.

And when the players are told they can't go away to play for more money, it's the same as telling a minor leaguer that he can't leave the "Pumkinsville Magicians" to go play with the New York Yankees or some other major league team.

From all indications, the rule is doing more harm than good. The fact that the greatest battery in baseball, Josh Gibson and Satchel Paige, are barred is proof enough. Together or separate, Gibson and Paige can draw more fans than any players in sepia baseball.

And without the healthy crowds, how do the owners of our teams expect to even approach the salary scales of teams in foreign countries? You tell me, I can't imagine.

"When Is a Bus Not a Bus? ODT and Baseball Moguls Start Figuring"

There was more than a little confusion at the Negro National League meeting in Washington last Tuesday when the Western Union boy delivered a telegram from the Office of Defense Transportation (ODT), which stated that no team would be permitted to travel by bus this season. The message of doom killed the hopes of every owner in the league, but the gentlemen took it the way housewives and taking rationing and the way most of us take things when we can't do anything about it.

At first, dejection filled the room when Secretary Cumberland Posey read the decree, but then somebody said something about cooperating with the government and being patriotic about everything else, and the suggestion was taken for what it was worth. Although one of the members mentioned later he wasn't sure it was worth all it was going to cost him, and that perhaps it would be best to just call it quits for the duration.

So now, it all adds up to one thing: Negro baseball will have to resort to the rods and rails this year, or there won't be any organized operations on the sun-tanned diamond front. Every team in the league has a bus to operate, but the ODT ruling instructs the owners to get rid of them as soon as possible. They will have to lease the buses out or Uncle Sam will take them over.

GOVERNMENT ORDERS LEAGUE CLUBS TO SELL BUSES IMMEDIATELY

"We will have to lease our buses out," Mr. Posey said with a sad note in his voice. "The Government needs buses to transport workers to defense plants, and we'll just have to cooperate."

That means that Messrs. Posey, Wilson, Gottlieb, Pompez, Manley and Semler will have to go out looking for bus customers right away. If any of you out there in the audience are potential bus buyers, these gentlemen of the Negro National League will welcome you with open arms, because from this date on, they will be riding the rails, if they do any riding at all.

The biggest problem confronting the moguls is the matter of railroad tickets. Although the railroads are doing a thriving business, greater than at any time in history, none of them have reached the benevolent stage wherein they are going around handing out free ducats to bus-less baseball teams. Consequently, the owners in the Negro National League are trying to figure out how they are going to ride around the country this summer with such a big overhead staring them in the countenance. You see, some of the owners are suffering from the shorts, which is another way of saying there isn't anything in their pockets to jingle.

OWNERS DETERMINED TO START
SEASON DESPITE HANDICAPS

So far, all of the teams intend to start when the season opens. How long they will be able to continue is still a very important question. The Homestead Grays, Baltimore Elite Giants and Philadelphia Stars should be able to play out the full schedule. However, the Newark Eagles, Cuban Stars and New York Black Yanks aren't so sure that they'll be able to stand the tariff that will be imposed upon them by traveling by rail. Everyone in the league outwardly appears optimistic, but there is a pessimistic atmosphere that is easily discernable and it will take some mighty big gates at the start of the season to inspire wholehearted smiles from the parties concerned.

It must be said, however, that the moguls are willing to gamble and risk their shining breeches for awhile anyway. All of the teams made money last years, and that fact alone is enough to convince them they should at least give it a fling this season. There is no doubt whatsoever that the public wants baseball this summer. Just how much they want it will be determined by the way they support the Negro National League and American leagues. By this time next year, Messrs. Posey, Wilson, Gottlieb, Pompez, Manley and Semler will be able to tell us just how much we want baseball. In fact, they may be able to tell us by the time the June moon comes up over the mountain because right now, they're singing that famous old ditty, "It All Depends on You!"

And they do mean ... *you*!

May 6, 1944

"Introducing 'El Diablo' Wells of Mexico"

MEXICO CITY, MEXICO—Senor Willie Wells, late of Newark, New Jersey, and now of Vera Cruz, Mexico, was tilted far back in the barber's chair. It was more than obvious that the dark-skinned Latin barber was a past master at shaving talking people, especially such talking people as Senor Wells, who was deep in conversation on baseball as it pertains to Mexico and the United States.

"I understand that there is a lot of adverse talk about me in the

States," Wells said, "because I quit the Newark Eagles and returned here to play ball. I hate that, but there's always two sides to any story."

While the artistic barber lathered the left side of Senor Wells' countenance, the stocky little shortshop, who is known throughout Mexico as "El Diablo," which means "the devil" in our tongue, gave his version of an issue that is hotter than a tamale in the vicinity of Newark, New Jersey.

"I came back here to play ball for Vera Cruz," Wells explained, "because I have a better future in Mexico than in the States. I wanted to stay and play with Newark because I consider Mr. and Mrs. Manley, the owners of the Newark team, fine people. But they couldn't offer me anything like I can get playing for Vera Cruz. Not only do I get more money playing here, but I live like a king."

The barber tilted Willie's tanned, square jaws and poised the blade for a very technical job around the vicinity of the neck. But that didn't stop Senor Wells from talking. "Some people look at my situation simply from the standpoint of money," he said. "But there's more to it than that. In the first place, I am not faced with the racial problem in Mexico. When I travel with the Vera Cruz team, we live in the best hotels, we eat in the best restaurants and can go any place we care to. You know as well as all other Negroes that we don't enjoy such privileges in the United States. We stay in any kind of hotels far from the best, and eat only where we know we will be accepted. Until recently, Negro players had to go all over the country in buses, while in Mexico, we've always traveled in trains."

In explaining the advantages of playing ball in Mexico, Wells pointed out that there is little difference between the life of a Mexican ballplayer and that of a big leaguer in the States.

LIVING LIKE A BIG LEAGUER

"Players on teams in the Mexican league live just like big leaguers," he explained. "We have everything first class, plus the fact that the people here are much more considerate than the American baseball fan. I mean that we are heroes here, and not just ballplayers."

The sparkling-eyed barber looked at Senor Wells as if he understood what the great Negro ballplayer was saying. After giving it due consideration, however, he decides he didn't and so continued with his work.

"Another thing," Wells said, "don't let anyone tell you that the owners of teams in the Negro league in the States can match salaries paid in the Mexican league. Newark offered me a nice salary, but there is no way possible that they can match what I am getting here. The Vera Cruz team, and other teams in the Mexican league, are sponsored by big companies or by wealthy men. If they want a ballplayer in the States, they can get him by simply overbidding American owners.

The barber waited patiently while Wells let go with the next mouthful of baseball chatter. "I was going to stay in the States and play for Newark," he said, "simply because I decided I'd like to stay home for a year. However, the Vera Cruz owners hoisted my offer so high I just couldn't turn it down. I agreed that the Newark owners have a kick, but I also think a ballplayer, or any working man, should take advantage of better opportunities. I didn't quit Newark and join some other team in the States. I quit and left the country. Seems to me I have a perfect right to do that."

FOUND DEMOCRACY IN MEXICO

"One of the main reasons I came back to Mexico," he said, "is because I've found freedom and democracy here, something I never found in the United States. I was branded a Negro in the States, and had to act accordingly. Everything I did, including playing ball, was regulated by my color. They wouldn't even give me a chance in the big leagues because I was a Negro, yet they accepted every other nationality under the sun."

"Well," the famed shortstop said, "here in Mexico, I am a man. I can go as far in baseball as I am capable of going. I can live where I please and will encounter no restrictions of any kind because of my race. So, you see, that also has a lot to do with my decision to return here."

The barber finished his important job, released Senor Wells from the chair and then turned to me with a sweeping grin on his face.

"El Diablo, El Diablo," he said with envious enthusiasm, and pointed to Wells at the same time.

"That means 'the devil' in Spanish," Wells explained. "That's what they call me here in Mexico. It's a pet name."

"Yeah," I said, "that's what they're calling you in Newark too, but they don't mean it the same way."

May 27, 1944

"A Rookie and a Vet Lead Hitters"

Pounding away at a terrific clip, James "Cool Papa" Bell of the Homestead Grays and Art Wilson, Birmingham shortstop, are leading the Negro National and American league hitters, according to the averages released this week by both leagues.

The 41-year-old Bell, whose star has been shining in the baseball heavens for almost 20 years now, is blasting the horsehide at a .583 clip, while Wilson, playing his first year in organized baseball, is going to town with a .452 average.

It is likely that the hot streak both men are enjoying will simmer down considerably as the season goes on and the pitchers will get the kinks out of their slingers. But right now, they are whaling the apple with great gusto and the opposition is certainly not at ease when they come to the plate.

The case histories of these two men are extremes. Bell started his professional career with the St. Louis Stars in 1922. For 10 years, he roamed the Stars' outfield and became known as the fastest man in the game. In '32, he went to Detroit to play with Cum Posey's Wolves, and the next year was with the Pittsburgh Crawfords. In 1937, he went to Santo Domingo, and in '38 through '41, galloped in the fertile outfields of Mexico. In '42, he returned to the States and played with the Chicago American Giants, and in '43, joined the Homestead Grays.

Bell was born in Stockville, Mississippi, is 5'11" and weighs only 158 pounds. He is a switch hitter, and from all indications, a mighty good one. In six games, he has connected 14 times in 24 attempts. He has scored nine runs. Four of his 14 hits have been doubles. He is tied with his teammates, Jerry Benjamin, for the lead in stolen bases with four, which means, of course, that despite his age, he's still carrying mercury in his heels.

WILSON WAS FOUND ON SANDLOTS

Art Wilson is a 21-year-old youngster who swings . . . very well, if you please . . . from the left side. This is his first year in the league, but you can bet your boots it won't be his last. The Barons picked him up on the sandlots of Birmingham. Manager Winfield Welch, a shrewd judge of ballplayers and a pilot of first rank, took one look at him and said, "Son, you'll do." And little Art is doing. He is 5'10", weighs 160 pounds and fields like a 10-year veteran. In seven games, he has come through with 13 hits in 24 trips to the platter. He has three stolen bases to his credit and has driven in two runs.

No one expects Wilson to continue his terrific pace. He's new in the league, and as soon as he gets around the circuit once or twice and the pitchers get a chance to examine him from the mound, they'll probably find he has a weakness. But, like Bell, right now you can fry an egg on him, he's so hot. And you can also get a happy greeting these days from Winfield Welch. Ain't Art Wilson his very own?

August 19, 1944

"East-West Star Dust..."

CHICAGO—The players from the East threatened to strike unless they were paid $100 each to play in the Classic. Saturday night, everyone was worried, the Eastern magnates in particular, because the National

League aces, including Josh Gibson, Ray Dandridge, Sammy Bankhead and others, vowed they wouldn't play unless the owners came across. President Tom Wilson quickly called a peace conference, and the players agreed to go through with the game... They agreed they couldn't disappoint 50,000 fans... American League players were given $100 and caused no worries... Sunday night, none of the Eastern stars could say whether they were going to get the money they demanded... Insiders claimed that Gus Greenlee, originator of the East-West Classic, founder of the Pittsburgh Crawfords and former president of the Negro National League, inspired the Eastern players to threaten a strike. Greenlee, it is alleged, met with a number of the Eastern players on Saturday afternoon and advised them to demand the money... Angry because, he says, the N.N.L. has been giving him the "brush-off" and refused him another franchise in the league, Greenlee came all the way from Pittsburgh to warn owners Posey, Jackson, Wilson, Manley, Pompez, Bolden and Semler that he's declaring a one-man war on them.

Busiest man here for the past two weeks has been Dr. J.B. Martin, president of the Negro American League... Everyone of any importance—and many not so important—were begging him for tickets... Box seats were sold out five days before the game... Vendors at the park made small fortunes... Duke Ellington, Bill [Bojangles] Robinson and Lena Horne's father, Teddy Horne, whooped it up for both teams... The press box was loaded with writers from out-of-town... Frank [Cleveland Call-Post] Young, Jr., whose father is Frank [Chicago Defender], did a great job handling the writers in the press box.

Ted Radcliffe, the "Birmingham Bomber," proved he's a great catcher. He was hurt while catching in the seventh, and had to be revived... Manager Winfield Welch wanted to take him out, but "Double Duty" said they'd have to call the police before he'd retire from the game. He went back in and finished... Josh Gibson's 440-foot double left everyone in the park gasping... When the ball headed for those centerfield bleachers, it was obvious no one could catch it... Consequently, everyone in the park, except the Western players, of course, hoped that he'd get a home run out of it... It missed a circuit by two feet, landed on top of the public address system and bounded back on the field... He got a terrific hand when he pulled up at second.

Sammy Jethroe pulled a boner early in the game when he misjudged Leonard's drive, but came back later with a beautiful throw to nail Gibson at the plate... Everyone agreed that classy, little Art Wilson of Birmingham has "it" plus... He played shortstop like a 15-year veteran... Dr. B.B. Martin, owner of Memphis, was all decked up in a spiffy blue sports jacket and white pants, while his brother, Dr. J.B., wore solid white, as usual... Gus Greenlee and William Harris, owner of the Grand Hotel, which was bulging with visitors and ballplayers, sat together in a box near the West dugout... Everyone looked twice at such beauties as Marca (Mrs. Joe) Louis, Mrs. Ernest Wright, whose husband bosses the Cleveland Buckeyes, and Miss Elizabeth Brammer of Detroit and West Virginia.

"They didn't send me here to pitch," Terris McDuffie, Newark ace, warned American League players before the game. "They sent me here to hit. I'm a slugger, I am." Then "Terrible Terry" lived up to his boasting by socking a triple the first time up... He died on third, however, as Mathis pitched brilliantly with the able advice of Ted Radcliffe... Tom Wilson of the Baltimore Elite Giants learned, much to his surprise, that two of his best players—Clark and Harvey, catcher and pitcher, respectively—had quit his team and joined Gus Greenlee's barnstorming Pittsburgh Crawfords... Harry Williams, manager of the New York Black Yanks, was one of the classiest dressers among the ballplayers, in his uniform in street clothes.

Conspicuous by his absence was Leroy (Satchel) Paige... He refused to play, and no one knew where he was... Celebrity-struck "goils" hounded the star players wherever they went... The game outdrew all games played in the majors Sunday... Mrs. Effa Manley, who runs the Newark Eagles, gave Terris McDuffie and Ray Dandridge a tongue-lashing for threatening to strike. "What the hell could I do?" McDuffie asked later. "I wasn't gonna be branded a strike-breaker. I had to be a union man, Suppose I had refused, The same guys I would be quitting were gonna play behind me in the game."... For the first time in many years, Alex Pompez didn't make the trip. He was in New York, where his Cuban Giants played at the Polo Grounds... Trains and buses were loaded... Wilbur Hayes won the prize for speed. He left Chicago early Sunday morning for Cleveland, where the Bucks played, and was back in Chicago by the time the classic was over. He hit the air lanes... Cum Posey, Gray's official, who has been seriously ill for the past two months, flew from Pittsburgh. Sunnyman Jackson, Posey's partner in baseball, did an oration in the Grand Hotel lobby on the sins of booking agents and what he would do to some of them if he had a good strong rope... Bessie Holloway of *The Courier* staff and now of Uncle Sam's WAC, arrived in time to see the game... Photographers were every place giving people the "flash-itis."

Everyone in Chicago, it seemed, tried to get in the Rhumboogie, Chicago nitery, on Saturday night... Hot spots were all loaded, and so were most of the patrons... Umpires Bluitt, McCrary, Moore and Cockrel worked like big leaguers... John Wright, pitcher for the Grays before he joined the Navy, was getting handshakes from all the ballplayers... He's a star pitcher now for the Great Lakes (Jim Crow) team... Duke Cumberland, Harlem Globetrotters' basketball star, sat on the best Western bench... Floyd Meadows, ex–All American at West Virginia State and now a "G.I.," saw the game... Whispers of a new league being organized for next year were all over the place... As was DeHart Hubbard, former Olympic broad jump champion, ex–University of Michigan track star, and now extremely baseball conscious... Elk officials were booming their big game here for next Wednesday night between Chicago and Memphis... Allen Page, regarded as the South's greatest baseball promoter, and the sports dean of New Orleans, was cornering owners for games and mapping plans for his annual North-South game in the Crescent City.

June 23, 1945

"Rain, Rain, Go Away, Little Alex Wants to Play"

DETROIT—Senor Alex Pompez, owner of the New York Cuban Giants and the cool Cuban from Havana, chewed viciously on his stogie and moaned a woeful tune as the rain came filtering down from overcast skies here at Briggs Stadium Sunday afternoon.

"Look!" wailed the handsome Latin. "Another Sunday of rain. I have never seen anything like it. These rains, they seem to be following the New York Cubans beisbol team every place. Three straight Sundays, we have been rained out at the Polo Grounds in New York, and now it is raining here." Obviously, Senor Pompez was more than het up over the unfavorable weather conditions. He is used to sunny days and balmy breezes of his beloved Havana. "I have never such weather since I started bringing teams here from Cuba more than 20 years ago," the Senor growled. "If these rains keep up, I am going to send the ballplayers back to Havana and bring over a swimming team. Personally, I do not like swimming, but I must put something in Mr. Stoneham's Polo Grounds."

No one can blame Senor Alex for dropping a few salty tears among the raindrops, because everything has gone against him so far this season. It seems that Mother Luck and Father Sun have, for some strange reason, given him the brush-off. When the season started, he had the best-balanced ball club in the Negro National League. He had an excellent pitching staff, a good infield, and a whale of an outfield. During the winter, he got the Polo Grounds' contract and everything looked rosy. But all that glitters is not gold. If you don't believe it, just ask Senor Pompez. His ball club is now cemented in the Negro National League cellar, and rain has forced him to postpone three of his big games in New York on successive Sundays.

"Not only am I having trouble with these rains," commented Alex, "but my ball club, she is suffering with injuries. I have the best team in beisbol, but we are never together so far this year. Right now, seven of my best players are hurt, and some of those who are playing are all bandaged up. My best pitcher, Dave Barnhill, has a sore arm, and six others look like they are veterans of World War II."

FEW CUBAN PLAYERS AVAILABLE...

"We look very bad today," the Senor moaned recently as the Birmingham Black Barons added their fifth run in the first game as against the Cubans' none, "because we do not have a real team in the field. We have pitchers in the outfield, outfielders pitching, catchers playing the infield, and . . . oh, everything, she is backwards! There are 14,000 people here this afternoon, and my club, she looks terrible! I do not like that. Always, I have been known to have a good beisbol team, and always I want one. People say, 'Alex Pompez always brings good beisbol teams to the States.' But today, they will say Alex Pompez does not bring such a good beisbol team to the States this year."

The dejected, despondent Latin was so perplexed he reminded you of a man facing the electric chair. "What should I do?" he begged with a helpless note in his voice. Why couldn't he send an SOS to Cuba for some help? Aren't there more Cuban players where these came from? "All the good players in Cuba are here in the States," he mumbled. "The big league teams are taking most of them now, and I have a very small field to pick from. There was a time when I could get all I wanted, but these Cincinnati Reds, Washington Sen-atoors, and minor league teams are taking them like anything."

"I guess I'll just have to wait until all my players get well," Pompez said. "That may be a long time, but I will wait. My first baseman, Dave [Showboat] Thomas, has been out for a long time now. He broke his wrist, and he cannot lift a bat or catch a ball. That is ve-ery bad. He is not only a crowd pleaser, but the key player in our infield. When he comes back, we will get going, but I don't know when he will return." The Senor puffed on his stogie, heaved a deep sigh, and added, "Linares has a bum ankle, Brooks has a bad leg, Scantlebury's arm is sore, Clark's arm is sore, and Noble has a broken finger. The whole 'dem' team is on crutches, and I am ready to go to the hospital from worry."

HE HAS A TEAM OF CRIPPLES...

As Senor Pompez gave out with his troubles, the rain started coming down in buckets. Umpire Pryor finally had to call the second contest in the fifth, with Birmingham leading 4–0. That was about as much as he could take in one day. "Once again, we are beaten by the rain," he said indignantly, "and once again, I am ve-ery unhappy. If this keeps up, I am going to buy a set of bathing suits. Maybe I should get some ducks and start a circus.

"If you know of any farmers who want rain," Alex said, "please tell them about my ball club. I will bring them to his farm for a small fee and guarantee him rain within one hour. We never fail. Our record stands for itself." Senor Pompez yanked his soft, brown fedora down over his eyes, gave his belt a rude jerk and started heading toward the dressing room. "I am going in here to see who got hurt today," he explained. "If this keeps up, I will have to put on a uniform. I can't get in the dressing room half the time for doctors, and we use so much rubbing alcohol, I run everytime I see a saloon. Why, one of my players used so much rubbing alcohol, he became saturated with it, and one day, he never showed up for a game. I was very mad when I caught up with him, and I demanded to know why he hadn't turned up that day. He said he smelled of so much alcohol that the man at the game at the park wouldn't let him in. The man said my player was drunk. Now, what do you think of that?"

There was never a better-liked man in baseball than Senor Pompez; and you cannot help but feel sorry for his plight. That's why everyone who knows him is pulling for him. They want to see him get a good break for a change.

As we left the park, Senor Pompez stopped to buy a paper. "What does it say about the weather for tomorrow?" someone asked. "What does it always say?" demanded the Senor. "Rain, of course!"

April 19, 1947

"Fans Plead for Jackie's Autograph"

BROOKLYN, N.Y.—The Brooklyn Dodgers has just blasted the New York Yankees, 14–5, in the first of a three-game exhibition series, and now the players on both teams were rushing madly for their respective clubhouses to avoid the maddening throngs it surged down out of the Ebbets Field stands and onto the playing field. Running off with the hordes of Brooklyn idols was a powerfully built fellow. There was a grin on his bronze face as he reached the dugout and disappeared through the tunnel that leads to the dressing room.

"Grab Jackie Robinson," cried a hysterical woman standing on top of the Dodger dugout. "Don't let him get away before I get his autograph."

Now, the maniacs were leaping over the box seat rail and trying to force their way past a squadron of policemen who were blocking the entrance to the dugout tunnel. "Please let me go through," begged a ruddy-faced youngster. "I promised my father I'd bring home Robinson's autograph."

But the big line of policemen refused to budge. They held the line, and now Jackie Robinson was safe in the clubhouse with the rest of the Dodgers. After a short wait, the guardian of the clubhouse door pulled it open and a battery of newspapermen and photographers swarmed into the room. The wave of heat from the shower room hit them full in the face as they marched through the fog of steam floating out of the showers. Jackie Robinson was sitting on a chair. One shoe was already off and both stockings rolled to the ankles. He was smiling happy and wiping his copper-colored brow with a big white towel.

"Well," asked one writer, "how does it feel to be a big leaguer?" Robinson's dark brown eyes danced happily and he smiled easily—almost gratefully—when he replied: "Gee, fellows, it's great!" The writers smiled knowingly and moved in a bit closer. Robinson's answer was an old one. He had said just what all rookies say their first day against major league competition. And they all smile, and they all seem just a bit awed at the thought of it.

"Were you surprised," another reporter asked, "when they announced you would play today against the Yanks?" In a way, that was an absurd question. Only 12 hours before this dark-skinned kid from Pasadena, Calif., had been a minor leaguer. He had been playing first base against the Dodgers. Only the color of his skin and the possibility that he might become a big leaguer some day made him any different than any other minor leaguer. Then suddenly he was no longer a minor leaguer. He became a big leaguer! Branch Rickey merely waved his fast, hairy hand—like a fairy godmother—and transformed him from a "busher" to the big leagues.

Was he surprised?

"Sure, I was surprised," Brooklyn's new first baseman said. "I was as surprised as I could be."

"Did you know it before they announced it over the public address system?" asked a reporter from the Associated Press.

"Oh, yes," Jackie said. "We had a meeting in the dressing room. We were all sitting there and Clyde Sukeforth was giving us a pep talk. He was saying that although this was an exhibition game, we have to play just as hard as ever to win it, because the Yankees have a good team."

The writers were scribbling madly now in their little pocket-stand notebooks. They were taking down everything he said like stenographers at a murder trial.

ASKS ABOUT JACKIE...

"Sukeforth was talking about the Yankees," Robinson continued, "and telling us how to play the different hitters, and telling the pitchers what to throw and what not to throw at certain hitters. Then suddenly, out of a clear blue sky, he stopped... He looked over the bunch of players sitting in front of me and said—'Robinson, how are you feeling today?' The question was popped so fast, I was startled at first. When I finally answered, I said I felt fine."

"Sukeforth said: 'Okay, then you're playing first base for us today!'"

One of the writers asked Jackie what he did then. "What did you do?" the writer asked. "That must have been a big surprise. Not too many hours before that you had been playing against the Dodgers, and now you were going to play with them."

Robinson thought for a moment. He seemed to be trying to get his thoughts in order, like a person who has been in a deep sleep and awakened suddenly. He draped the big white towel around his shoulders and burst out laughing. It was great hearty laugh.

"Why, I just sorta' gulped," he said.

"You gulped?" two or three asked at the same time.

"Yeah," he said, rubbing his throat as if to show them where it happened. "I just gulped."

Robinson then sat down and started to take off the heavy, woolen stockings that all big leaguers wear.

"Were you frightened when you walked out on the field to play against the Yankees?" he was asked.

"No, I wasn't," he said quickly. "I felt real good. Before the game, a number of the Brooklyn players came up to me and shook my hand. Fellows that I played with last year in Montreal like Tom Tatum, Dixie Howell and some others shook my hand and congratulated me. They said they were glad to have me on the team."

By this time, the photographers were taking over. Robinson had to put most of his uniform back on so he could pose with Clyde Sukeforth, who has been directing the team since Durocher left.

PRAISED BY SUKEFORTH

"He's going to be all right," Sukeforth assured the audience. "He's a great ballplayer and will prove it as soon as he gets adjusted. He can hit, run and field. He's a great all-round athlete and can't miss."

Finally, some of the commotion died down and Robinson got a chance to slip into the shower room and bathe. Not long afterwards, he was dressed and ready to leave. But when he emerged from the dressing room, he was mobbed by fans who had been standing outside. With considerable modesty, he agreed to sign score cards and other such autograph treasures. He politely acknowledged that he knew or remembered the countless admirers who came up to him and said such things as: "Say, don't you remember me, I'm Jim Smith from the Coast. I met you when you were at U.C.L.A." Although he only remembered a few, Robinson played his role perfectly, because he didn't want anyone to think he'd forgotten them. "Sure, I do," he'd say. "That was a long time ago, wasn't it?"

When he finally reached the street, he was mobbed again. There seem to be 1,000 people standing directly outside that door. When he stepped out, they gave him a deafening roar and surged upon him. Despite the efforts of another squadron of police, he was absorbed in a sea of slapping hands and was literally carried away. Flashbulbs were exploded with machine-gun-like rapidity and the whole world seemed to be screaming in unison: "Jackie Robinson!"

He finally made his way to the car that was to take him to his hotel. But it was a hard struggle. They almost pulled his clothes off him. They pushed him in all directions at the same time, trying desperately to get his autograph. They screamed and hollered like people who had escaped a concentration camp. They stepped on his feet and some begged him to merely cast a look in their direction.

"That's the price of fame," someone said as he climbed into *Courier* photographer Billy Rowe's automobile.

"Yeah," Jackie said with a deep sigh of relief. "Boy, they really swamped me, didn't they?"

"Well, you're a big leaguer now, Jackie," somebody else pointed out. "They're your fans and the people who pay your salary."

"Yep," the Brooklyn first baseman said, "and I love 'em. Every darn one of 'em!"

And that's the story of Robinson's first day in the major leagues.

FRANK A. YOUNG

Chicago's Boss of the Sports World

Small stories reveal a lot. Take Frank A. "Fay" Young, the first dean of black baseball writers, who is said to have known in his 50-year career every important black athlete of the day, mostly through his role as sports editor of *The Chicago Defender*. In an October 1970 *Ebony* story, A.C. "Doc" Young (no relation) described a visit to the office of the venerable writer.

"It was cluttered with wall-to-wall paper," he wrote. "I ... started to pick up a sheet of paper that had fallen, I thought, to the floor. Fay Young caught me in the act and warned me not to touch it. I was about to tamper with his 'filing system.'

"'I know,' he said, 'where *everything* is in this room.'"

Another story appears in *The Defender*'s November 1957 obituary of Young. Russ Cowan wrote that while he was covering a game at the old Schorling Park in Chicago, "a discussion came up after a Detroit base runner had been hit by a batted ball as he ran between first and second.

"One of the younger writers did not believe the batter should be given a hit," wrote Cowan. "'Give the batter a hit and credit the second baseman with a putout,' Young replied tersely. 'You young fellows should read the rule book and learn something about the game.'"

That was Young: gruff, to the point, and, according to Doc Young, "an institution" of black sportswriting. "Medium-sized, bespectacled, always immaculately dressed and sometimes caustic of tongue," wrote Young, "he was a one-man sports department.

"He was justifiably proud of his position, if unwisely selfish in the operation of his department.... [He also] worked himself to a frazzle in an individual capacity when, I'm sure, he could have had it much easier, and increased his influence even more by hiring a staff."

Frank Young was a pioneer. The country's first full-time black sports writer, he joined *The Defender* in 1907, just two years after Robert S. Abbott launched the paper in a friend's kitchen and opened the first office in

Frank A. Young (photo courtesy The Chicago Defender*).*

rented space on State Street. The contents of that first office were spartan: a card table and a borrowed chair. *The Defender*'s first issue was printed on credit, since Abbott's total capital at the time was 25 cents, needed for paper and pencils. But by 1915, the paper was a hit, with circulation of 230,000.

Young's career grew accordingly. And it didn't stop at baseball; indeed it spanned thousands of sporting events, including heavyweight title fights, track and football, all chronicled weekly for 30 years in his folksy but sharp columns, usually called "Fay Says." In addition, Young picked an annual All-American black college team and was a founder of the Tuskegee (Alabama) Relays.

There are countless examples of Young's generosity to students— "hundreds of times," Cowan said, he extended financial aid to a student having difficulty in meeting the board bill or paying tuition.

"Oh, he would grumble and one would believe he was the meanest fellow in the world, but deep down in his heart there was a soft spot," Cowan wrote. "It could be reached by anyone" with a needy story.

Young spent his entire career at *The Defender*, except from 1934 to 1937, when he was managing editor at *The Kansas City Call*, another black paper. He was also *Defender* managing editor from 1929 to 1934.

Like other writers of the era, he occasionally crossed the line into an official capacity with organized baseball. Young served five years as Negro American League secretary and later as director of publicity.

Two days before Young died at the age of 73, he was in the *Defender* office to submit his column, "Fay Says." After his death, co-workers found this note: "You don't need to get the ticket for me for the fights Wednesday. I'll be out of town."

The pieces that follow were all written for *The Chicago Defender.*

September 9, 1939

New York had an East versus West game. The official paid attendance was a bit over 12,000. That looked like a sack of gooberpeas in the huge Yankee Stadium. There are several reasons for such a small crowd. In the first place, the East has educated New York's baseball fans up to expecting four-team doubleheaders. To have one game on a Sunday afternoon, after several four-team gala bills, naturally left the fans believing they would be paying a price for one-half of what they had been used to getting. The fans, once given a bargain bill, expect bargains to continue.

★   ★   ★

Mrs. Abe Manley, who owns the Newark Eagles with her husband, usually does a lot of talking. While in Chicago, she opposed and argued against every move that helped put 32,000 paid admissions in Chicago on Sunday, August 6. But the fortunate part of Mrs. Manley's arguments was that the other club owners ignored her.

Some of Mrs. Manley's objections, as well as some of her arguments are, as Shakespeare said in *The Merchant of Venice*, "like two grains of wheat lost in two bushels of chaff, you may seek all day ere you find them—and when you have found them they are not worth their search."

★   ★   ★

Jimmy Powers, sports editor of *The New York News,* wrote a nice column the morning of the game on Sunday, August 27, advising baseball fans (and I am presuming he was speaking to the major league fans) to journey out to Yankee Stadium to see the All-Star players in action, many of whom were barred from the major leagues because of their color.

All that was fine on the part of Mr. Powers, but the white people in New York evidently didn't give a tinker's damn about Negro baseball or better yet—the All-Star game—because out of millions of souls, the best the game drew was a few. More too, when Mr. Powers' article appeared on Sunday morning, the folks had already made up their minds where to go and most likely were on their way.

Harlem, with its 275,000 or more of our group, ought to have had a better representation. And where were the folks of our race who live in Brooklyn, Jersey City, Orange, New Jersey, down on Long Island and Philadelphia? Either the game was not publicized right or something is radically wrong.

Mrs. Manley, who strenuously objected to the cost of publicity for the game played in Chicago, probably has a change of heart by now, if that is possible, and will admit that the course pursued in Chicago for six years has brought people through the turnstiles, whereas the miserly methods pursued in the promotion of the New York game left Yankee Stadium three-fourths empty.

*   *   *

The Chicago game taught the promoters a lesson. Of the 32,000, less than 1,500 were white baseball fans paying their way. In other words, the success of the game was made by Negro newspapers and the daily press. Even as liberal as they were here, it didn't put people in the gate. It was the Negro press that carried the percentages, the feats of the various stars all through the year, and it was the readers of the Negro newspapers who had the knowledge of what they were going to see. Folks came from Elkhart, Indiana, Indianapolis, St. Louis, Kansas City, Gary, Indiana, Milwaukee, Detroit and Louisville to see the Chicago classic. Even with these, the greatest part of the crowd were the Chicago fans.

The Negro press has been more than fair with Negro baseball, but some like Mrs. Manley, are not fair with the Negro press.

August 2, 1941

The ninth annual East versus West classic is history and the East now leads in number of games won, five to four. Sunday, July 27 was a banner day in Negro sports history. Fifty thousand fans watched the "dream game" at Comiskey Park, Chicago. It was the largest crowd to ever attend a sport event in Negro history.

The game brings out several things worth commenting on. First is that the people will pay to see the attraction *if* they know they are to get their money's worth. Second is Negro baseball will pay—and Sunday's crowd of 50,000 didn't have 5,000 white people out. The crowd was as orderly as any crowd of 50,000 could have been.

★   ★   ★

However, it was very surprising to see some of our so-called intelligent people become so ignorant of other people's rights. Men and women got in the wrong box seats and because they held box seats for another, refused to move. And some never moved regardless of the pleadings of Andy Frain's ushers who became disgusted and quit trying to straighten out the trouble. The truth of the matter is there were not enough ushers to handle that crowd—and there were not enough policemen.

★   ★   ★

The East versus West game ought to make Chicago folk get busy and have a ball yard of their own. Why is it we have to "rent" the other fellow's belongings? Many get married in a "rented" tuxedo or full dress suit. That suits that individual, but it is not at all surprising when people who go to this East versus West game can't agree with the enormous amount of money paid for the rental of the White Sox park that ought to go into something of our own.

And what makes it all the more sickening is the fact that this year, the Chicago American Giants have played but three games in Chicago and have but one more to play—that for the benefit of Providence Hospital on Sunday, August 31, when Satchel Paige will return here. The Chicago team is unable to build a park.

★   ★   ★

The public was fairly well satisfied with the game with the exception of those who wanted the West to win. But even they were satisfied when Satchel Paige finally went to the mound in the eighth inning. There were many who knew that each pitcher could hurl only three innings. They wondered why Paige was not sent in to pitch the seventh. They are still wondering.

So are we.

Many in that crowd were attracted by the publicity given Paige. After such a build-up, it seemed to be a wise thing to use Paige three full innings. After all, the public must be satisfied. I am still answering phone calls and answering questions as to why Paige was held put. "I don't know."

*   *   *

The game had its good points and a lot of bad points. The East, like last year, had too much defense in that infield. Take Dick Seay of the New York Black Yankees off second base and Felton Snow of the Baltimore Elite Giants away from third and yank "Rabbit" Martinez of the New York Cuban Stars out of shortstop and then go and hide Buck Leonard, the Homestead Grays first sacker, and the West might have scored some runs. Snow and Seay robbed West batters of hits, both pulling down two line drives with one-handed stabs.

The East had an outfield too. Oh, forget the ball that Kimbro of the New York Black Yanks lost in the sun because even Joe DiMaggio will lose them in that spot in the Sox park. Roy Campanella, Baltimore, caught the entire nine innings for the East.

As for the West, there was but one serious mistake made. When Hilton Smith left the game, Bankhead of the Birmingham club could have gone to the mound. That is second guessing. Ted Radcliffe, called "Double Duty," played in, although knowing what Leonard is weak on. Folks are wondering "how come the home run?"

*   *   *

Six runs in one inning don't look so hot for any all-star combination. It doesn't please the West's followers. Some are criticizing the fact that at one time, there were four of the nine West players in Memphis Red Sox uniforms, There was Jelly Taylor at first, Neil Robinson in center, Radcliffe pitching and Larry Brown.

The crowd was appeased when Satchel Paige went to the mound and struck the first two batters who faced him.

Terris McDuffie, Homestead Grays, who hurled the first two innings, was the winning pitcher. Overcome by heat, he was unable to go to the mound in the third and Impo Barnhill relieved him. Hilton Smith, Kansas City Monarchs, was the losing hurler. Newt Allen, the Kansas City shortstop, was forced from the game when overcome by heat.

There was one double play in the game that 90 percent of the fans didn't see. That was Campanella to Martinez.

*   *   *

Five thousand fans were in the Sox park before 11:30 A.M. It was a grand day with the thermometer at 83 degrees at 7 A.M. On the field during the game, it must have been 112 degrees. The players who have been in South America said they had never suffered with the heat to that extent before.

Then to make matters worse, the ceremonies before the game came near spoiling everything. The flag raising as Miss Julit Rhea sang "The Star-Spangled Banner" was great. Then came a long-winded speech that caused thousands to become restless because these folks came to see a ball game and not hear any race problem address that might have been all right on the street corner two miles away. The folks came to see a ball game, forget what race they belonged to, and here it was like being dashed into your face like a pail of ice water. Whoever was responsible for it ought to be given one good swift kick in the pants. It's plain damnfoolishness and folks don't pay $1.10 and $1.65 to hear it.

And as we sign off, let's hope that West will trot out a victory team next year and not have the East say after the game is over that the West had a better team on the bench than they had on the field—and "had a team on the bench that might have been able to beat us."

September 6, 1941

Jackie Robinson "did his thing" in the All Stars versus the Chicago Bears game at Soldier's Field last Thursday night. The 37–13 score doesn't begin to tell him how Robinson did all that was expected of him and more too. He is the first Negro to score a touchdown in the eight games played. The 98,203 paid him a tribute as he left the field.

Robinson represented the University of California at Los Angeles. Last year, Kenny Washington of the same school played for the All Stars against the Green Bay Packers. The longest return of a kickoff is down in the books behind Washington's name. He ran one back 88 yards last year.

★   ★   ★

The game ought to make the United States Army and Navy wake up. Every time a Negro who is qualified asks to join a particular branch of either service, there is a cry that Negroes and whites can't do this or that together. A great example of what can be done is shown in this College All Star versus pro game for charity. Men from all sections of the country were on the Bears' team. Since professional football draws the color line when it comes to players, no Negro was with the Bears. But the Bears played against Robinson and marveled at his ability. The Green Bay team played against Kenny Washington in 1940 and the New York Giants played against Bernie Jefferson of Northwestern and Horace Bell of Minnesota in 1939.

What the pros need to do is to look at that 50,000 crowd that watched the East versus West All Star baseball team at Comiskey Park in July. Maybe the Cardinals or the Bears could use an additional 10,000 each time they play here. One thing is certain: 10,000 times whatever the admission price is not to be sneezed at.

★ ★ ★

Twelve thousand watched Satchel Paige turn back the American Giants last Sunday for the benefit of Providence Hospital. Mrs. R.A. Cole and her committee deserve much credit for a crowd that big because some bad mistakes were made in the promotion.

In the first place, the date was a poor one. It had been picked and the game advertised before Mrs. Cole knew that she was to be general chairman of the game committee. Any Sunday that is before a holiday is a bad day because people take advantage of the Saturday, Sunday, Monday weekend and hit the country.

Advertising "Satchel Paige to pitch all the way" wasn't the wisest thing to do. It only recalled that Paige pitched but two innings in the 1941 East versus West game when a great portion of that great crowd of 50,000 was out to see Paige hurl. Although the rules, like the white All-Star baseball game, allow a pitcher to work three innings, fans had expected Paige to work the three innings. He didn't and lots of folks stayed away Sunday because they had no assurance that he would pitch. Baseball managers failing to use their noodle can get folks down on them.

Paige pitched six innings Sunday. He didn't pitch all the way and no sensible baseball fan expected him to do so when he pitches nearly every day.

Again, no one can assure any crowd that any pitcher will "pitch all the way." The first window cards put out never said whom Paige was to play with or against. Additional cards had to be printed informing the public.

Providence Hospital made some money, but about one-half of what it might had if the date had been ideal and promotion handled a bit differently. At that, hats off to Mrs. Cole for the ability to "save the day."

May 23, 1942

KANSAS CITY—Every time Felix Payne, Q.J. Gilmore and the writer get together, it is a rehashing of ball games of days gone by. Then add Dizzy Dismukes, now manager of the Kansas City Monarchs and Frank Duncan, veteran catcher of the same club and throw in Newt Allen, and you've got a quorum.

We were sitting in Cleve Ransberg's cafe over some juicy steak and onions when the subject of shortstops came up. The entire Kansas City aggregation was arrayed against me for a time. There were such players as the late Moore and the late Mendez of the Kansas City Monarchs, both of whom were rated tops when it came to shortstops. We admitted such but stuck out to the last that we knew one who was better than either of the men mentioned.

★   ★   ★

We allowed our hearers to scratch their heads and then blurted out "John Henry Lloyd" of the Lincoln Giants, American Giants and Bacharach Giants' fame. They said, "You got something now." We knew it.

Well folks, John Henry Lloyd turned 58 years old the 25th day of last month. He lives in Atlantic City where he is employed as a janitor at the Indiana Avenue School. He settled in the seashore city 11 years ago.

There's a long story behind Lloyd and his 44 years of baseball. Back in 1918 and thereabouts, we called him the second to Hans Wagner. He fielded like Hans but was a better hitter.

The youngsters around the schoolyard all call Lloyd "Pop." They love to gather around him and listen to his stories of baseball as played in days gone by.

★   ★   ★

Lloyd still plays baseball, sharing first base duties in the Johnson's Stars along with a youngster young enough to be his grandson. Except for a tired expression around his eyes and a wrinkle or two, John looks about the same as he did 20 years ago. He had the same old smile when we last saw him.

John Henry Lloyd was born in Jacksonville, Florida, in 1884. He played school baseball between the ages of 14 and 18, then he got a job as a red cap. Thus he came in contact with many traveling teams. He soon joined the Cuban Ex-Giants who had on its rolls the late Rube Foster and others who late made Negro baseball. He started his professional baseball career as a second baseman, but as the years rolled in, Lloyd was better at shortstop where he was second to none—white or black.

On his last birthday, Whitey Gruhler, sports columnist in *The Atlantic City Press-Union* wrote:

"In a series of 13 games between the Almondares club and the Detroit Tigers in Havana, Cuba, Lloyd compiled the highest batting average, outhitting such stars as the great Ty Cobb, Sam Crawford, Matty McIntyre, George Moriarty and others. His average for the series was .500."

In an old issue of *Esquire Magazine,* an article by Alvin F. Harlow, dealing with the great Negro baseball stars, disclosed that a well known St. Louis baseball writer, interviewed on the air, was asked the following question:

"Who do you think is the greatest player in baseball?"

The writer's answer was:

"If you mean the greatest in organized baseball, my answer would be Babe Ruth. But if you mean in all baseball—organized and unorganized—my answer is John Henry Lloyd, a colored man."

July 24, 1943

Satchel Paige will be named as one of the pitchers for the West in the 1943 East versus West game. Paige says he is 37 years old. He was born in Mobile, Alabama. His mother, Mrs. Lulu Paige, still lives in Mobile.

Along with Fred McCrary, who is one of the umpires in the East versus West classics, Pete Clay and L.C. Gurley, Paige was a member of the Chattanooga Lookouts in 1926. Paige's folks tried to get him to go to Tuskegee Institute, but Paige didn't see it that way.

He joined the Birmingham Black Barons, then owned by R.T. Jackson. Jackson sent to Dolphin, Georgia, for one George Perkins who had been doing the receiving for the Montgomery Grey Sox. Perkins was at that time perhaps the best showman of the Negro catchers.

★   ★   ★

Paige and Perkins remained with the Black Barons until 1929 when the famous battery was broken up. Paige joined the Baltimore Black Sox in 1930 and played for that club for one season. He joined Tom Wilson's Nashville Elite Giants, then playing out of Cleveland. In 1931, Gus Greenlee took Paige to pitch for the Pittsburgh Crawfords.

Gus had a publicity man by the name of John Clark who stood well with the Associated Press and the daily sports scribes of Pittsburgh. Paige's pitching got plenty of press notices. His salary with the Lookouts was $200 per month plus expenses. His salary with the Black Barons was $275. With the Black Sox, owned by a white man named Rossier, Paige drew down $400. Greenlee paid Paige $550 and all expenses. Greenlee secured Perkins who by that time had played on several clubs in the old Negro National League, a catcher for Paige. Perkins was paid $400 per month.

Paige remained with Greenlee for five years and then jumped to South

America. In a trade, Greenlee turned Paige over to the Newark Eagles. Paige returned to the United States and has played with the Kansas City Monarchs since.

★   ★   ★

The greatest single drawing card in baseball today, Paige is the highest paid Negro ballplayer. Sometimes, he receives as high as $1,000 for pitching part of a single game. We have known the time when his day's work brought him a check for $1,500.

Clark Griffith, owner of the Washington American League club, will attest to that fact. In a discussion, J.L. Wilkinson, owner of the Monarchs, told Griffith that he paid Paige more money than Griffith paid his highest paid ballplayer. When Griffith tried to laugh it off, the laugh was cut short. Paige happened to walk into the office to talk to Wilkinson. Wilkinson asked Paige to show him the check he had given him for the game he had pitched against the Homestead Grays about an hour previous, and Paige pulled out the check. It was for $1,500.

Paige pitched five innings Sunday, July 18 at Wrigley Field, Chicago, allowed no hits, no runs, fanned seven, got credit for a 1–0 win and received $2,000.

Paige has some memorable games that he likes to recall. Once, when he was in South America, his team won and Paige left town by airplane to get away from the natives who had bet on the losing team. Then, the elongated hurler recalls that he beat Bob Feller two out of three games, winning the rubber game 6–3. And Dizzy Dean has quit trying to beat Paige and his mates. Out of 12 games, Dizzy has one win over Paige, a 1–0 contest in Kansas City.

He had fanned Joe DiMaggio several times. "They all look alike when I'm right," Paige declares. Right now, he has become interested in his chickens. He owns one rooster and a half dozen hens. "But you wait, I'm going to have a real chicken farm one of these days," the great pitcher said.

Paige never complains about autographing anything the fans poke before him. He is a candid camera addict. And what "burns him up" is the other camera fans who tire him out posing for shots and never send him any. "Gonna call a one-man strike one of these days," Paige said.

"Wait, don't go yet," he yelled at your columnist. "Put this down and don't forget it." Paige knows how to hit, don't forget that. "And when it comes to laying down bunts, I take the prize for that too."

We agreed with him. He does.

June 9, 1945

Jesse Owens, holder of the world's broad jump record, a leap of 26 feet, 8 and ¼ inches, made at Ann Arbor, Michigan, in the 1935 Big Ten meet, was to have, according to the advance publicity sent out from Louisville, runs against a race horse as an added attraction to a baseball game. Owens, it will be remembered, equalled the world record in the 100-yard dash, established a world record in the 220-yard low hurdles [this was later broken] and set a world record in the 220-yard dash all in that one afternoon.

Owens, we understand, graduated from Ohio State University sometime after his glorious triumphs in the 1936 Olympics in Berlin, Germany, when Hitler congratulated all the victors, but suddenly made his exit rather than shake the hand of the non–Arayan Owens. That's all past history. Hitler is now supposed to be dead and Owens, although gainfully employed, continues to perform for a promoter who gets part of Owens' share of the receipts, and, to our way of thinking, both Owens and the promoter are sealing a black eye to Negro baseball.

★   ★   ★

Owens has a right to do as he pleases as an individual. He was once a salesman for a liquor company on the strength of his athletic fame, although he specifically stated that he, himself, didn't drink. We do when we want to, but we wouldn't appear as a salesman for the same and tell the youngsters we didn't drink, nor would we be a salesman for the same and hobnob with athletes as an example for the youngsters. Owens was severely criticized for so doing. Then he got himself another position—but he continues to exhibit his athletic prowess, which to us is all right—but not against race horses.

We cannot pretend to be anything but against any man running against a race horse whether that man be Jesse Owens or Luke McGluke. Consequently, we aren't even pretending we are neutral in the matter. We are dead against it.

Alfred Loisy, in writing to Pope Benedict XV during the first World War declared, "Whoever pretends to be neutral in matters where justice is concerned fails to be impartial. As a matter of fact, whoever pretends to be indifferent is in reality siding with him who is in the wrong and against him, who is in the right."

As the old gent down home would say, "Them's our sentiments exactly."

★   ★   ★

Columnists find it hard sometimes to speak out because when they battle for this or that cause or question or problem, there are too many who are quick to draw the conclusion that they do so in order to profit by it, or to create a sensation, or to satisfy a secret ambition, or to draw attention to themselves.

On the other hand, a straight-forward conscience cannot always be at peace with all men. When a man once finds himself at peace with the world, he had better examine himself and ask himself to which of his obligations he has been unfaithful.

In our severe criticism of Owens, we are faithful to the Negro baseball fans, the public in general, and to the great number of athletes who are record holders.

April 13, 1946

That was Cum Posey.

And now he is no more.

He left this world like the lived ... asking no favors. That was the way Cumberland Willis Posey, owner of the Homestead Grays, died in Homestead, Pennsylvania. On Monday, April 1, the city schools of Homestead closed in honor of Posey, who was a member of the board of education there since being elected in 1931.

To Ira F. Lewis, veteran newspaperman and president of the Pittsburgh Courier Publishing Company of which Posey was a stockholder, Posey had declared that he prided himself on never being a good loser. "Good losers are seldom winners," he told Lewis.

*   *   *

Posey's fame ran all the way from Canada to Mexico into Puerto Rico and South America, where various members of his team went to play ball in the winter months. From the Atlantic to the Pacific, there was but one Cum Posey—just like there was but one Rube Foster in the latter's heyday. Posey and Rube were friends sometimes and again they were unable to agree. Rube at that time was for organized baseball and Posey was a fly in the ointment. Then when they got to Posey in the fold, he was wont to kick over the traces. Of course, there was trouble.

Posey was for a winning ball club—one that won all the time. We never saw him sad, except when the Grays went down to defeat.

The last football game we worked with Posey was the Morehouse versus Bluefield game back in the late 1920s, in Columbus, Ohio, on a Thanksgiving Day. He was head linesman. The line and backfield coaches of Ohio State were referee and umpire.

We've seen him when he was a wizard on the basketball floor and when he was a thorn in the side of the old St. Christophers and the Incorporators of New York City. It took the great *Chicago Defender* five of Sol Butler, Bobby Anderson, Hubbard, Blueitt and company to worry the Leondi club of Pittsburgh. The feud was a humdinger. It was East against West with the West never bowing. When basketball history is written, Posey and the Leondi club that succeeded the Monticello Delaneys, will have a very important place.

★   ★   ★

Few knew Posey coached the Homestead High School teams in basketball and football. Few knew he was a letterman from Penn State, who, at one time, attended Duquense.

True, the world has lost a man who made himself famous in three branches of sports. But it it also true that it is a sad state of affairs when both friends and enemies wait until that man dies before they will admit his true worth.

Posey and we disagreed many times. He always said we were for the Negro American League and the West. Sometimes, he'd hop on us through his column but never with any spleen—simply a difference of opinion. Then he'd meet us and we would shake hands. His only excuse would be. "Well, that's the way I thought it at that time," and laughingly would add, "You know there ain't no way for me to rub the doggone thing out."

★   ★   ★

There won't be those familiar arguments over the merits of the East's teams in the East versus West classics—if there are any, they won't be the same as if Posey was there.

He'll be missed at future Negro National League meetings. He was secretary. He will be missed at the joint meetings. He won't be there to say, "You sit down, doggone it, you haven't got a thing to do with it," and 10 minutes later would have cornered us in the hallway with, "you know, you know," etc.

But he had a way, even when he became overwrought, of never falling out with you. He had a way of making his enemies respect him and sometimes winning them over as friends. As for his friends, he could rely on their loyalty. He had a forceful way of making you agree with him.

That was Cum Posey.

And now he is no more.

★   ★   ★

April 13, 1947

Jackie Robinson was purchased outright by Branch Rickey, Sr., president of the Brooklyn Dodgers, on Thursday, April 10 in the middle of the ball game between the Montreal Royals and the Brooklyn Dodgers. It was a straight cash deal with other players going to the International League club.

The decision received the approval of all the coaches as well as Leo Ernest Durocher, then manager of the Brooklyn team. Rickey, often referred to as "The Brains," held a secret conference with his coaches at his Forest Hills home on Wednesday night. He found them in one frame of mine — to bring Robinson into the Dodger fold.

Rickey couldn't make up his mind. Then, in the middle of Thursday's ball game, he made a decision that will go down in history. We recall our interview with him last June in his Brooklyn office. He said then that Robinson would be given every chance to make good. Rickey kept his word.

Robinson, who played in the Negro American League in 1945, batted .349 to lead the International League in batting in 1946. He was named the best defensive second baseman in the league. Then, on the suggestion of Durocher, Manager Clay Hopper, who hails from Mississippi, switched Robinson from second to first base against the Dodgers in spring training. Jackie's record for the 13 exhibition games against the Dodgers in Panama and Havana was .340.

★   ★   ★

It is hoped that the Negro fans, who want to see Robinson remain in big time baseball, will learn to treat him as another top-notch ballplayer. He should not be made to carry the added burden of "the race problem" on his shoulders. He will have a hard enough job playing the brand of baseball expected of any other big leaguer.

Two things are important. The first is the conduct of the Negro fans. Drinking is out in all National League parks. Profane language, if you have to use it, should be reserved for your home where your wife can "brain" you.

Robinson will not be on trial as much as the Negro fan. The Negro fan has been the "hot potato" dodged by managers who would have taken a chance by signing a Negro player. The unruly Negro has and can set us back 25 years.

Jackie will be here on May 18. We hope that Sgt. Harnes and "Two-Gun" Pete and some other brave Negro policemen will be assigned to the Cubs' park. Harnes and "Two-Gun" know the hoodlums. This situation shouldn't be, but it is.

The second thing is that Robinson is against being singled out before a game to be called to home plate and presented with numerous gifts. There will be eight other Dodger players in the game. Jackie insists on being treated as a ballplayer trying to make good and not as a Negro player seeking special privileges.

The Negro fan can help Robinson. The Negro fan can ruin him. Robinson is an ex-army officer, a ballplayer and a gentleman. Let us try and meet his qualifications as a gentleman. If you Chicagoans have got to raise a lot of hell and do a lot of cussing, go somewhere else.

August 21, 1948

Ol' Satchel Paige returned to Chicago Friday night, Aug. 13 and was the magnet that drew 51,013, the largest night crowd in White Sox history. Fully 20,000 were turned away. At least 20 were injured when those milling about the front entrance tried to jam their way past the turnstiles at Comiskey Park.

Paige crossed up the baseball experts, who were of the belief that he could go but five to seven innings, and pitched the entire game, giving up five hits and blanking the tail-end Sox. Paige's team, the Cleveland Indians won 5–0, and moved back into first place in the hot American League race. He made his Chicago debut as a Negro major leaguer in magnificent style.

On Tuesday, Aug. 3 in Municipal Stadium, Cleveland, Paige was the magnet that drew 72,434, the largest crowd to ever attend a night game in Cleveland. It had been announced the day before that Paige would start. Likewise, on Friday, the Chicago dailies announced that Paige would start that night in Comiskey Park.

IMPROVED PAIGE

Friday, the 13th, didn't bother Satchel—neither did the White Sox. He didn't walk a batter. He didn't try to strike out everybody. He was a showman, second to none, but at the same time, he was much improved over the Satch who used to fling them over in the Negro American League of the Kansas City Monarchs.

He was more than the Satchel who pitched the East to a 1–0 victory over the West as a member of the famous Pittsburgh Crawfords, and more than the Paige who beat the East as a member of the Monarchs, or the Paige who didn't get into one of the recent East versus West games because he wanted 10 percent of the net and declared he would give it to charity.

Ol' Satchel got even with the Negro baseball heads by drawing a larger crowd than the East versus West game. He looked at the jam-packed Comiskey Park and smiled as he recollected that he had hurled many a night game there, and it was as familiar to him then as it was years ago. Same old park, same lights, bigger crowd, same home plate, everything the same except Satch was now in Big Time baseball.

The 51,013 loved him as much as Satchel loved the limelight. But the old master had learned a few things. There were eight other men out there and a corking good field general in Lou Boudreau, manager and shortstop for the Indians.

During the early innings, Paige would flip the first ball across for a strike. In the closing frames, he changed it and the first ball he threw was a "ball." He bent over long enough to be sure he had the right signal from Catcher Jim Hegan. He drew a big laugh from the crowd when he snapped a throw to second in an attempt to catch a Sox runner who was taking too big a lead.

DOBY SCORES

Larry Doby, first Negro to be signed in the American League, tripled to center in the Cleveland fifth. Ken Keltner struck out, but Hegan flied to Seerey in left and Doby scored the first run of the game after the catch.

Doby, who can run about as fast as Jackie Robinson, stole second and third. He scored one run and got two hits in four times at the plate. He made three catches in the outfield, one of them a corker.

Cleveland added one more run in the eighth and three to salt the game away in their half of the ninth. The victory was the fourth for Paige against one loss. It was the second time he had started a game.

Take no credit away from Sox pitcher Randy Gumpert, formerly of the New York Yankees. He fought it out with Paige for eight innings, giving away to a pinch hitter. Although Moulder finished and three runs were made off him in the ninth, Gumpert was charged with the loss.

Until the sixth, Paige didn't allow a man to reach second. Up to the sixth, only Luke Appling in the first, and Philley in the sixth, nicked Paige's delivery for hits. Two were out each time.

Gumpert opened the sixth with a single and went to second on a sacrifice, but the Sox weren't able to do anything with Satchel's offerings. Peck gathered in Lupien's fly and Boudreau tossed out Appling.

The crowd rose en masse to give Peck a great hand as he came in for the Cleveland eighth. In the seventh, he backed up against the right field wall to take Aaron Robinson's long drive with his glove hand.

JOE BOSTIC

A Crusader of His Time

Joe Bostic's prose, like his newspaper, was a full frontal assault against the injustice of Jim Crow America, circa 1940.

"I was one of those people who constantly contended . . . that the Negro National League and the Negro American League were playing better ball than the majors," Bostic said in a 1973 interview with *Black Sports* magazine. "And as proof, Jackie Robinson went in, took baseball apart as a one-man show. Simply because he knew how to bunt, he knew how to steal bases and he knew how to excite."

Bostic spent the most productive of his sportswriting days at a strident paper of the mid–1940s, *The People's Voice* of Harlem. Owned and published by the controversial and flamboyant preacher-turned-congressman Adam Clayton Powell, Jr., the paper clearly stated its opinion right on its masthead: "A Militant Paper . . . Serving All People . . . The New Voice for the New Negro."

The slogan fit. Powell called his own weekly column "The Soapbox." His entire paper, which had a relatively brief run from 1942 to 1947, anticipated the kind of militancy of the future Black Power movement. When the newspaper ran excerpts from Richard Wright's novel *Native Son,* now a classic of American literature, so many readers protested about the language and style of this realistic tale of poverty and crime in Chicago's black community that only four installments were ever printed.

As *People's Voice* sports editor from 1942 to 1945, Bostic mixed it up week after week with the major league baseball establishment. His biggest moment came in April 1945, when he escorted two Negro League players, Dave "Showboat" Thomas and Terris McDuffie, to Dodger sprint training camp at Bear Mountain, New York, and demanded tryouts for them. Details of the encounter were laboriously written up in *The People's Voice.* Although Dodgers' General Manager Branch Rickey permitted the tryouts, neither player received a contract with the organization, and Bostic, as he sarcastically admitted years later, was branded as a "fresh nigger" and excluded from team news coverage.

Rickey's position on the tryouts was that Bostic had backed him into a corner, "without having given time for him to canvass the 16 owners, to find out what they should do in a case like this," Bostic recalled in 1973.

"So, we went to lunch [whereupon] Rickey and I sat in the middle of the Bear Mountain Inn, and he cried and told me about his lack of prejudice, and how, as a manager of his college, that they went to play somewhere and their opponents didn't want to play because his team had a black player," Bostic added. "And he actually had roomed with the fellow because nobody else would room with him.

"And then he came up with a classic quote. He said, 'Look, you're pretty cute.' I said, 'No, I'm not cute. I'm not concerned with being cute. I brought you two ballplayers.' He said, 'Yes, but if I give these men a tryout, you've got the greatest sports story of the century. And if I don't give them a tryout, you've got the greatest sports story because it's an absolute showdown. I don't appreciate being backed into this kind of corner.'"

Bostic, like many of his peers, had an active media career, but a relatively short one as a baseball columnist. In addition to sportswriting, he was at various times a gospel music disc jockey and promoter, a boxing and baseball announcer and a Manhattan-based theatrical agent, credited with bringing Mahalia Jackson to New York. He was also sports editor of *The Amsterdam News,* for which he occasionally wrote a column, and the first black admitted to both the Boxing Writers and Track Writers associations.

Born in Mount Holly, New Jersey, and raised in Atlantic City, Bostic was a 1932 graduate of Morgan College, now Morgan State University, where he played baseball. After graduation, he became the first black announcer at WCBM radio in Baltimore, and attended for a time the Columbia University Graduate School of Journalism.

Later, Bostic was a popular disc jockey in New York on WLIB radio, where he conducted the "Gospel Train" program for many years. He even found the time to found a Brooklyn private school, the Junior Academy. Small wonder that when he died at 79 in 1988, he was hailed by *The Amsterdam News* as a pioneer.

So how rare was Bostic the black sportswriter in America in the 1940s? "Completely, like something off the moon or something, because then you had nothing going for you," Bostic once said. "You had no sympathies, you had no radio or television or black movement or the desire of whites to placate us. It was like digging a career out of concrete."

The following stories all come from *The People's Voice.*

Joe Bostic, circa 1943 (photo courtesy Lee Bostic).

March 21, 1942

"Dreamin'"

The other night, *Scoreboard* was reading a series of articles dealing with the figures of the new loans to the Allies, the daily cost for the prosecution of the war and the latest national appropriation. This, plus an admixture of ribs, pie, whipped cream and pickles set the stage for one of the strangest dreams ever recorded. It went something like this:

We suddenly found ourself with piles of green stuff before us, in the front office of a thriving business. There was a line of men outside the door waiting, nay pleading, for us to open the joint. When we went out to take a gander at the sign to see what kind of business we were in anyhow, there was the sign that said clearly:

BOSTIC & CO. BASEBALL PLAYER BROKERS

Now, it was all clear to me. Those men outside, who were now milling about in the shop, were owners and managers of major league baseball talent, the Negro stars, who would be available this season to replace the many who had gone to the armed services. And this operative had thoughtfully tied up all of this talent, which, of course, now was worth a king's ransom.

First came Joe McCarthy of the New York Yankees, looking for a seasoned third baseman, as he was afraid that the youthful and inexperienced Gerald Priddy might not be up to the job of filling adequately the ailing Red Rolfe's shoes. So, I sold Ray Dandridge of the Newark Eagles for a paltry $25,000. (Sorry sir, no checks; cash only and in $1 bills.)

Next came bashful Mel Ott of the Giants, complaining that he was on the spot in this, his first year, but he felt that, given an infield, he could give New York a team that would easily finish well up in the first division. Yes sir, we have just the thing in a smart package buy, and if you take all four you can get a bargain. So we gave him Showboat Thomas, Dick Seay, Jesse Williams of Kansas City and Jake Spearman for $85,000. Mel couldn't get the money down fast enough for fear I'd change my mind, and when the deal was closed, he went singing out the door as he turned dozens of cartwheels (knocking the protesting Bill Terry flat on his fanny in the process) and rushed to a phone booth to tell the papers that his worries were over.

Larry MacPhail wanted *two* pitchers to insure his club's repeating for the pennant, so we let him spend $18,000 for Jonah Gaines and Hilton Smith, throwing in Henry McHenry so that he'd have a hitter in the bargain. Boy, was he tickled at that deal?

At that moment, in the door walked the one man I'd been waiting for, Cy Slopnicka of Cleveland. Yeah, I knew he wanted a Sunday pitcher to replace Bob Feller, who is in the service, and there was no need to bicker, for I had laid away something special just for him. It was a little number tagged Satchel Paige and all I was asking was $32,863.79 (tax included). He could take it or leave it—no other offers considered. Pshaw, he took it so fast that he didn't wait for the 21-cent change from the odd dollar. Manager Lou Boudreau was tickled silly.

Now, I was about to make my kill. After selling Sammy Hughes to Detroit to replace Charley Gehringer, I set up a deal to sell Jerry Nugent the entire Homestead Grays' club as a unit to replace the Phils and the Elites to Washington for a cool $250,000. Then the roof caved in.

Coming across the street were four men, and not one was smiling. "Well, gentlemen," I said, "what can I do for you?" The answer, in unison: "Nothing."

The first gent introduced himself as Mr. Thurman Arnold, who said he was connected with the government and he handed me a true bill charging me with the operation of a trust and a monopoly, with an injunction restraining me from further operations. The white-haired tall one said that his name was Landis and that I was about to ruin the great American game by bringing in these American Negroes and thereby establishing an undesirable precedent in introducing the democratic theme into the lily-white baseball setup. The third man, a Mr. Tom Wilson, said that he was the president of the Negro National League and if I persisted in taking players from his league, the investments of the club owners would be jeopardized. Dr. J.B. Martin explained that he held a similar position in the Negro American League, and that he felt in effect the same as Mr. Wilson. Then they scooped up all of the money, let Josh Gibson and the rest of the players out of the padlocked cages in which I was keeping them, and told me if I didn't get the hell out of there, they'd break my neck. I protested that the Landis setup was a monopoly too and an un–American one at that. And that a fellow had to turn an honest dollar. But they'd hear none of it and together, they tossed me out onto the sidewalk.

Well, anyway, thought I, it was some racket while it lasted, and as I thought over the reports of what the Cubanolas had done to the Dodgers during the training season, this thought stood out:

They got themselves shoved around by fellows who made up the second weakest team in the Negro National League. And La Crux, who starred against them, was up three years ago and couldn't make the grade.

July 11, 1942

"In Re Negroes in Big Leagues"

Sooner or later, every sportswriter, particularly the column caliphs, gets around to discussing the proposition of Negroes playing in the so-called major leagues. Now, with the war situation and its democracy theme a springboard for many "beefs," this question has taken on the status of a "cause" with a great number of individuals, organizations and movements. Since every Negro sportswriter in the country has let fly with an opinion on the subject, it was only natural that it would be just a matter of time before *Scoreboard* would be smoked out as to where it stood on this much-discussed issue. Thus far, we've kept (so we thought) tactfully quiet on the proposition for the very simple reason that our notions about the whole idea don't exactly see eye-to-eye with the popular point-of-view. And if a writer is to maintain any smattering of friendship and respect with his half-dozen or so readers, one of the surefire ways is to be on the popular side of all controversial issues. Knowing this to be the case, there is no reason why said sportswriter should ever experience anything but sweetness and light in his relationship with his readers. But me—I'm a semi-nincompoop with an iconoclastic complex, so it's small wonder that I extend my neck as a target for the scythes in the hands of the reading head severance experts. So, here we go on our foolhardy way!

• Our approach to the question is strictly mercenary.

• We're deadly practical about the entire situation.

• We're not convinced that the baseball played in the organized leagues necessarily represents the best caliber of ball played per se, and therefore, the Negro players would not be moving into faster company than that in which they were already playing. So, let's get to sortin' the potatoes.

Baseball is strictly big business and any calculation in regard to the racket must always use as a consistent denominator the predominance of the profit motive in the dictation of any policy. Thus, anyone attempting to read democracy or sportsmanship into the basis of conduct of any of the league policies is slightly off-center. An outstanding example of this approach is the business of "spring training" trips. Here is a cute dodge pulled off behind a curtain of ostensibly conditioning the athletes, which is nothing more than a newspaper space grabber at a cost much below the line rate insertion for display advertising for the amount of space given. Since all baseball prognostications are made under the sign of the dollar mark (and this is accepted as being OK, even to the extent of a presidential endorsement of the gag), why shouldn't the fledgling that is Negro organized baseball take the same attitude? The whole discussion breaks down into the query, "Would Negro baseball profit or lose by the entry of Negroes into the American and National leagues?" *Scoreboard* feels that the net result would be written in red ink on the ledgers of Negro baseball.

Why? Well, let's figure in the first season of the experiment that three Negro players went into the major leagues. So, we're going to be very generous and assume that they would get $15,000 each—a total of $45,000. That item is covered by the East-West game alone, which gives you an idea of the immense financial return of Negro baseball in any given season. Make no mistake about it, the entry of even *one* player on a league team would serve completely to monopolize the attention of the Negro and white present followers of the Negro baseball to the great injury of the Negro baseball exchequer.

Today, there are two Negro organized leagues, just as the threshold of emergence as real financial factors. Organized Negro baseball is a million-dollar business. To kill it would be criminal and that's just what entry of their players into the American and National leagues would do. And don't give me that guff about the white minor leagues because the situations are not the same. Nor should money from the byproducts be overlooked such as the printers, the Negro papers and the other advertising media, which get their taste; the officials, scorekeepers, announcers, secretaries and a host of others. These monies now are coming into Negro pockets. You can rest assured that we'd get none of those jobs in the other leagues, *even with a player or two in their leagues.* We control—or could, if some of the owners would stop "Uncle Tomming"—the vast revenues and byproducts accruing from Negro baseball. And, I submit that it would evaporate with the diversion of interest and resultant diversions of patronage as the result of a few Negroes going into the other leagues.

On the second count of practicality, why subject any player to the humiliation and indignities associated with the problems of eating, sleeping and traveling in a layout dominated by prejudice-ridden southern whites! Don't forget, there is *now* a Jim Crow seating policy in St. Louis. A more practical suggestion would be the admission of an entire Negro-owned, controlled and personalized team into one of the leagues of we just must play in their backyard. Then all of the money and jobs from there would come to us.

And about the caliber of play, the only evidence thus far submitted shows that the Negro players have more than held their own when playing against the white leaguers. Further, the powers that be in those leagues tacitly admit the potential excellence of the Negro teams by refusing to play them intact. They only go for "all-star" games and exhibitions. And if they think that they are really the world champions and have a right to the title, then I dare the winner of the World Series to meet the winner of a series between the Homestead Grays and the Kansas City Monarchs for the real undisputed title. Until that time, there is no proof that the white leagues' caliber of ball is superior over Negro ball. If you or they think so, then what about the Renaissance basketball team?

In sum: From the idealist and democratic point of view, we say "yes" to Negroes in the two other leagues. From the standpoint of practicality: "No."

Dissenters' line will please form on the right, but first you must disarm.

August 14, 1943

"The East-West Classic, Top Sports Event"

As we've intimated on a half-dozen occasions in these dispatches, the pilot of this space is a sports enthusiast of the first order and an incurable fan, not to mention our being a charter member of the Grandstand Managers' Association. In other words, we are a thoroughly impressionable young man—definitely of the gee whiz crowd.

Knowing this about me, it shouldn't be too hard for you to understand my being overwhelmed by the magnitude and the potentialities of the annual East-West classic held annually at Comiskey Park, Chicago, as I consider the game in retrospect from my journalistic cubbyhole back here in New York.

These are some of the thoughts that run through my mind as I reflect on the Chicago Classic: This is not only the biggest Negro sports event, but the largest single proposition in the nation from the point of view of patron interest to the extent of paying an admission price... No other event begins to draw anything like this one... 51,723 *paid* admissions... The nearest that we've come to it in New York is the 29,000 at the Satchel Paige game at Yankee Stadium last summer and the slightly better than 20,000 who tried to get into Madison Square Garden for the Freedom rally a couple of months ago, and that's not even close... The "take" is close to $60,000, which comes under the head of high finance in any league... Pleasant to report that the spectacle is singularly free of rowdyism in the stands. Maybe we should import the Chicago fans here in order that they'd give some of the ruffians who attend Yankee Stadium games, a lesson or two in behavior.

We got a terrific thrill when given the honor of introducing the Eastern standard bearers over the public address sytem to that throng that packed and jammed every available inch of the huge sports amphitheater... Biggest ovation went to Josh Gibson, power hitter... He didn't get a homer, but came through in the ninth inning clutch with a sizzler through short that all but tore off Jesse Williams' arm.

Quite an argument in the press box on the play in which Howard Easterling had an easy out of a base runner coming into third on an infield tap. Thinking that there was a force play at the base, Easterling merely touched the bag with his foot and made no attempt to tag the runner, who, of course, was safe. This writer, along with Art Carter and several others, insisted that the third baseman should have been charged with an error.

The opposition, led by Bill Nunn of *The Pittsburgh Courier,* who steadfastly contented that the base runner had gained the base by virtue of a steal, credited him with a stolen base and let Easterling off without an error... But section 9 of Rule 70 says in part: "An error shall be given for each misplay that prolongs the time at bat of the batsman or prolongs the life of the base-runner or allows a base-runner to make one or more bases when a perfect play would have insured his being put out." Our contention was and still is that the third baseman should be charged with an error because he certainly failed to make a perfect play... What do you think???

The game is a monument to the imagination and creativeness of the late Roy Sparrow, who along with Gus Greenlee, conceived the game... An outsider is appalled by the fact that the owners, booking agents and others who share in the money, haven't seen fit to declare Greenlee in on the proposition. Either it has been overlooked or else there are some unusually ungrateful people associated with baseball. I prefer to think that it is the former, and I fervently hope that the dereliction will be amended before another East-West game is played... It is patently clear that the Negro interests are gradually losing control of the promotion—if indeed they haven't done so already... Seeing the boys operating at the game or least some of them—it wasn't too hard to understand.

The officiating of the game was strictly big league... So good in fact, that you were hardly aware of the presence of the umpires on the field, and that, in the final analysis, is the acid test... The East team was actually an augmented Homestead Grays' club ... such an arrangement seems to this column to miss the whole purpose of the game: to increase fan and player interest in organized baseball as represented by the two leagues... Maybe we're dumb, but we can't see why it wouldn't do more good all around if each club was permitted at least three players to help make up the squads... As a case in point, certainly if the West squad included Goose Tatum, whose sole job was to entertain the fans with his pre-game antics at first base, then the East squad surely should have included Jim West and Showboat Thomas to name two. It is a great thing this classic, and I, for one, am proud to be a part of it.

May 6, 1944

"Whither the Black Yankees?"

Well, we've had a look at the New York entry in the Negro National League and it's painful to report that the loyal New York fans are getting shortchanged again with the current edition of the New York Black

Yankees. We don't know what the answer is to the riddle, but this we do know: that it would be beneficial to everybody concerned if New York had a good ballclub, as indeed it should, since this is the big town. Last year when we wrote that money might be the solution via the purchase of some much-needed ballplayers, our good friend and Yankee owner Jim Semlar called this sentinel severely to task. We accepted the censure in the spirit in which it was given. Now, another year has rolled around, and little or nothing has been done about the miserable club wearing the spangles of the Black Yanks.

Genial Jim can reprimand me unendingly for taking a critical attitude toward our home club if he chooses, but you can't kid the fans. The fact was pointedly brought home Sunday afternoon when the fans began leaving in droves late in the first game of a doubleheader, and at the conclusion of the second game, the stands were virtually deserted.

It has been called to my attention that I shouldn't forget that I am employed by the Yanks among other teams in the league as the Yankee Stadium announcer and therefore should soft pedal all criticism. Well, there are two arguments against that thesis. First, I'm a New York fan and I want my town to have a winner: yea, I *Demand* it or hate the inalienable right to beef loud and long as to the reason why. Secondly, as a newspaperman with even an ounce of integrity, I owe it to my readers to call 'em as I see them or suffer the humiliating alternative of having the age-old indictment of the Negro press hurled at me, to wit: Negro sportswriters don't know what the hell they're talking about.

I know there's a war going on and that the manpower shortage is acute. Still, I note with dismay that other clubs can find men. As a case in point, the Homestead Grays came up with a new shortstop to replace Jelly Jackson in Joe Spencer; a new pitcher, Dave Hoskinds who beat John Stanley in the second game; and Dolly King, a New York boy stolen out from under our very nose. The Cubans have gone out and dug up a new star in Gil Garrido plus *two* West Indian players to draw the Island fans. Newark has several new and capable replacements for men gone off to the wars and so on down the line.

It's an indisputable truth that every ballplayer would like to play in New York. Then, it is strange indeed that our Black Yanks have so much trouble ensnaring a few. Terris McDuffie is presently trying every known maneuver to get traded *away* from New York. Make sense?

There are no ways about it, the fans aren't going to support such as we saw Sunday, and the sooner the folks up in the front office realize it and make some move toward remedial action, the better for the fans, for Semlar and for the league. That is unless somebody hopes to see the Cubans hog the whole show, the fans, the money, the popularity *and the pennant.*

We want a team worthy of our fidelity and our support. Is that asking too much Soldier Boy?

August 12, 1944

"Satchel Paige Bucks the Wheel— and Not Too Smartly"

CHICAGO—We landed here last Wednesday for a quick visit and thought we might as well knock off a pair of pigeons with the same slingshot. Accordingly, we started to make a few routine sports calls on some of the newspaper and promotional key folks who make sports go in this town. Well children, never in my born days have I ever seen such an apparently calm surface covering such a tempest as currently is raging on the Negro American League (Western) front. The surface picture gives every indication that the town—and the baseball folks—are complacently planning for the annual outpouring of fandom for the East-West game when some 50,000 of the faithful shoehorn themselves into the pews at Comiskey Park.

⋆   ⋆   ⋆

Great source of contention and precipitator of a terrible epidemic of frayed nerves and bad tempers is the highly publicized Leroy "Satchel" Paige. And it's that disappropriate amount of publicity, the fault of near-sighted operators, which has given Leroy the exaggerated notion of his importance that has resulted in the present impasse and ridiculous quarrel. But, I'm putting the dray before the sulky, therefore it would probably make the gab a little more understandable if I gave you a quick reap of what's transpired to date. Then, maybe we can find the noggin or noggins on which should rest the blame. We might also get a fuller picture of the deep ramifications and repercussions that are more or less certain to result from the present flareup.

Last year, Paige, who unquestionably is one whale of a drawing card, received some $800 for his brilliant three inning hurling chore in the East-West classic. According to Dr. J.B. Martin, the league president, this was made up from the contribution of $50 per club with the balance made up by Tom Baird and J. Wilke, owners of the Kansas City Monarchs. Throughout the season, this same hurling ace had been paid a percentage off the top and it was only natural that he should expect the same pattern of payoff in the classic. Now, let's not lose sight of the fact that this game is played by the greatest stars of the two leagues—each the unquestionable kingpin at his position in the loop with which he's affiliated—yet their stipend by no stretch of the imagination matches that of Paige.

This year, the solons decided that the all-star game was just that—an aggregation of the greatest stars. Therefore, Paige's bid for a percentage was denied. Paige, seeing this turn of events, then offered the counter proposal that the game be played for a war fund and that all receipts be turned over thereto, in other words, Paige's position was that if I can't have a special lion's share then no one gets anything.

And then at this point, Paige's story that he won't play in the game unless it's a 100 percent charity venture appears on the pages of every Chicago paper and gets released by the major wire services. This, however, not until after President Martin had decreed that Paige's name was to be stricken from the Western roster and he was not to play in the classic.

Knowing that Paige himself would hardly have taken his case to the papers for such orderly news releases, informed baseball folks hereabouts detect in the operation the fine hand of Abe Saperstein, top booker out this way. Saperstein was relieved of the publicity job for the game this year and these astute baseball people following the "misery loves company" line of reasoning figure that the fellow guided Satch through the linotype maze. By getting this adverse publicity for the classic, which pictures Paige as a charitable martyr, they reasoned that shrewd Abraham could thus strike back effectively without showing his actual hand.

Pieced with the action taken by the Negro National League against playing under Saperstein promotions, this firing of him from the spot in the classic may be the beginning of the long threatened bolt toward Negro control of Negro baseball.

Is Satch to blame for believing that he is bigger than the game? I think not. The shortsighted but unimaginative magnates have steadfastly refused to exploit other stars so that there was more than this single attraction or box office "name." This because they didn't want other men to make real money. They simply created a Frankenstein that got well out of hand. This is a big gamble for Satch to take. If the game is a sellout *without him,* he'll be in a tough bargaining spot in the future. And it's 6-2-even-odds that they will sell out this Sunday. As for Saperstein, who has been fulsomely praised by conferees Dan Burley and Wendell Smith, this is but the first round. He still holds the aces of promotional rights in most of the major league parks here and westward.

That, m'heaties, is a terrific hump for the magnates to get over before they're in a position for a showdown fight.

If, indeed, that's what they sincerely want.

I'm just wondering.

April 14, 1945

"Dodger Tryouts Blow
at Jim Crow Baseball"

WEST POINT—Here in the tradition-rich setting of the United States Military Academy last Saturday, the turning point in a great battle was reached—the battle to open the doors of the great American game of baseball to all American citizens, including Negroes—when the ever-colorful Brooklyn Dodgers gave a tryout to two Negro players. This history-making development came 24 hours after this writer had taken the two men—Terris McDuffie, pitcher of the Newark Eagles and Show-boat Thomas of the New York Cubans—to the Brooklyn club's training camp at Bear Mountain, New York, and asked for a tryout for them. General Manager Branch Rickey, who conducted the tests, refused to say whether the men would be considered for Dodger berths. In fact, he flatly told McDuffie that he would not make a committing answer.

This epochal break in the stonewall of baseball Jim Crow came with dramatic suddenness after 36 hours of whirlwind activity that had started with our party's arrival at Durocher Field at Bear Mountain.

Our party consisted of the two players; two other newspapermen, Jim Smith of *The Pittsburgh Courier* and Nat Low of *The Daily Worker,* and this writer.

On arriving at the field, I asked Harold Parrott, the Dodgers' public relations man and secretary, for an audience with Rickey, after telling Parrott that I had brought along the two ballplayers for a tryout. Parrott said that Rickey could not be disturbed as he was watching an intra-club game, but would probably talk to me later.

About 15 minutes later, Parrott returned with Bob Finch, the elderly assistant to Rickey, who talked to us for fully an hour explaining that I should have advised the management of my intended visit. Because it was irregular, I was told that it would be impossible to get the men a workout since the only men permitted to work out were those who had been seen and recommended by club's scouts and then received invitations. He went to great lengths to impress on me the unbiased attitude of the Dodger officials and to convince me that they were men of good will. I then asked how was it that those coots had never seen a Negro player worthy of recommendation. This questions he said he couldn't answer.

Shortly thereafter, we were told that Rickey wanted us to be his luncheon guests. We accepted this invitation.

RICKEY CONSENTS TO WORKOUT

It was during the course of this luncheon that I was able to get from Rickey an assertion that he would look at the players. He said that he would personally look over McDuffie, but he would have to assign Thomas to someone else. Pinned down, he said that he would see him at 11 A.M. Saturday. After a press conference with the metropolitan writers covering the team, we left.

On Saturday morning, we returned for the 11 A.M. appointment. After an interminable wait, Rickey sent for me to join in the morning press conference. Smith and Low also later joined.

We then came here where we met Rickey, Manager Leo Durocher and Coaches Charlie Dressen and Clyde Sukeforth, as well as virtually the entire newspaper contingent awaiting the planned tryout.

At 1:25 P.M., Thomas and McDuffie emerged from the dressing room in the West Point Field House, wearing Dodger uniforms and entered the playing cage to get the workout started. I introduced the men to Durocher formally. Rickey then sent them to jog around the field by way of getting warmed up. They were next told to limber up by tossing the ball around for about 10 minutes.

McDUFFIE PITCHES

Rickey then called Sukeforth to take his place behind the plate and called McDuffie to start pitching. After he had thrown a half dozen or so pitches, Rickey started calling for the kind of pitches he wanted thrown. McDuffie was sharp as a whip and was splitting the plate on pitch after pitch. Once he was underway and the tension eased off, he worked as smoothly as a newly oiled diesel engine. Now, Rickey was shuttling back and forth from the mound to behind the plate and audibly marveling at the control Mac was exhibiting.

THOMAS BELTS 'EM

Thomas was called to bat against a speedy lefthander, which put him at a distinct disadvantage since he is a leftie himself. But he still belted plenty of them for what would have been long safeties in any outdoor field.

When it came McDuffie's turn to bat, he strode to the plate with that consummate self-assurance, which is his hallmark. He slammed several to distant points, thus making good his boast to Rickey of the day before that "I'm a hitting pitcher."

Both men had three turns at bat, and at the conclusion of these turns, the most momentous single adventure in the fight of Negroes for entry into the major leagues was concluded. History had been made—encouraging history at that.

"It Seems Rickey, Alone, Was on the Level"

Within the space of 48 hours last week, *Scoreboard* had a chance to get an authoritative picture of the real thing and attitude of two groups of baseball executives in the noteworthy experiment of changing the national pastime from a Jim Crow setup, the Dixie tradition, to a democratic one operated in accord with the code of good sportsmanship. We saw and talked first-hand with two sets of men who had been the subject of opposite types of operation.

On the one hand, there were Willard Brown and Henry Thompson, who had been caught in the cheap, dollar-hungry operation of the management of the St. Louis Browns. On the other hand, there was Dan Bankhead, as the second spoke of Branch Rickey's wheel of integration and a sterling example of what can happen when someone is really levelling. In this case, that someone was Brother Rickey, and it's for that reason that we here are furnishing a 21-gun typewriter salute in his favor.

I think at the outset, I should make it clear that there is no love lost between Rickey and Bostic, so this piece is hardly a matter of back slapping for a personal friend. The Mahatma has never gotten over his pique against this writer for having called a showdown three years ago when we took two men to the Dodger spring training camp at Bear Mountain and secured the first official tryout of any sort ever given to Negroes in organized baseball. That was one concrete maneuver that gave the fight its biggest push. Despite the claims of a number of folks, the record shows that from that day at Bear Mountain, the campaign to get Negroes into the big leagues, long simmering, really started to boil and never stopped until the goal had been realized on the same team, where we started the action—the Dodgers. Rickey said at the time that we took unfair advantage of a situation and its new value by coming to the camp unannounced. He further charged that we violated a confidence by informing the newspapers of the proceedings when it was his desire to conduct the token tryout in comparative secrecy. So you can see that not too much brotherly love burns in the Rickey heart for sports scribe, Bostic.

The feeling is just about mutual on our part. We aren't an enthusiastic rooter for the Rickey technique. We resented his implication that we were dishonest and will continue to do so until such time as we receive an appropriate apology. We are further resentful of the fact that he had Clyde Sukeforth call us on the telephone at our home to get the lowdown on some eight or nine players then under consideration, plus seeking further recommendations. Since the Dodger management had sufficient confidence and respect for our knowledge of Negro baseball and its players to seek our estimate, it burned us up that Rickey didn't have the courtesy to give us the credit publicly instead of pretending that these prospects had been scouted for two or three years, or that some newspaperman recommended the men to him. I merely point out these feelings to make it clear that the reason I'm pitching for BR is because, no matter what my personal feelings toward him, you have to admire the honest and decent way he has handled the men involved in his operations funneling Negroes into the Dodger organization.

From the very outset in the Robinson case, Rickey made it definitely clear that the then crude and untried Robinson seemed to have the abilities that would be used to advantage in the building of a Dodger pennant machine. Never once since Jackie made that auspicious debut in Jersey City one bright afternoon last summer, has the Mahatma veered from the established course that he has chartered. Certainly during the early part of the present campaign when Robbie was awkwardly unfamiliar with the first base job and for a spell found it tough to buy a hit at any price, there was ample opportunity for the Brooklyn boss to say he had made the big effort in good faith, but found that the candidate just wasn't of big league caliber and tossed him over after milking all of the box office potential out of him. Instead, Mr. Brooklyn stood steadfastly by his convictions as to the man's ability and was paid handsome dividends—both at the box office and afield where Robbie has become an important and key man in the determined bid of the Flatbushers for the National League flag. How can you fail to look with admiration upon a man with that kind of loyalty to his convictions?

While officially there was never a boycott against the entry of Negro players into organized baseball, everyone the least bit conversant with the situation knew there was a close knitted understanding among the owners to keep the sepia superbas on their own side of the Jim Crow fence. But, by the same token, there was a pretty general off-the-record dislike of Rickey by his fellow operators, a dislike born of jealousy over the man's shrewd ability to mine plenty of gold out of the baseball hills and to manufacture pennants at ridiculously low cost because of his farm system—a product of his amazing organizational ability. So it meant that Rickey has to further risk antagonisms of his competitors by embarking on his racial program. Adventurer that he is, as long as the adventure is basically sound from a business point of view, he was the first to sense the inevitability of the eventual break in the wall, and accordingly, got the jump on his sleeping and prejudice-minded fellow operators. But, it took plenty of guts to face the ridicule on one hand and snide insinuations on the other, that he had violated a sacred "agreement" that was in the form of an understanding.

It is in the opinion of the writer that some specific and concrete cognizance should be taken of the job Rickey has done. Therefore, *Scoreboard* makes this specific recommendation:

That the sports fans and a comprehensive citizens' committee give him the most impressive inter-racial testimonial dinner that this town ever saw. We hereby invite such figures as Mayor O'Dwyer; Brooklyn Borough President John Cashmore; Bill Robinson; Judges Jonah Goldstein, Myles Paige, Frances Rivers and Hubert Delaney; Parole Commissioner Sam Battie; Broadway columnists Walter Winchell, Dorothy Kilgallen, Leonard Lyons, Ed Sullivan, Damon Walker, Earl Wilson, Louis Sobel and Lee Mortimer; newsman Dan Burley, Bill Chase, Rick Hurt, Billy Rowe, Buster Miller; Brooklyn's number one lady, Lena Horne; and all other civic sports, journalistic and political leaders in this town to head a committee to pay a deserved tribute to a man, who, in our estimation, has struck the most important and significant blow for sports democracy in the past 20 years. Naturally, this paper and this column will offer every cooperation and facility at their command to put over such a project.

Well, there you have it with our sentiment, friends, because we think the man, friend or not, deserves demonstrative recognition.

CHESTER L. WASHINGTON

From Writer to Millionaire

For Chester L. "Ches" Washington, it all started with a typewriter. "I had always been fascinated by the typewriter and would often stay late after school typing," Washington recalled years later. "I figured this would be a skill my father would approve."

As a college student in Virginia, Washington learned to stroke the keys at the rapid rate of 139 words per minute. His speed served him well, for in a short time he parlayed that skill into what would be a long, distinguished career in journalism. Of his many accomplishments in the field, Washington was perhaps best known as the millionaire publisher of the Wave Newspaper Group, a Los Angeles–based newspaper chain.

Along the way, he became the first black member of the *Los Angeles Times* editorial staff, once scored an exclusive interview with Fidel Castro in Havana, and even had a golf course named for him. He was also Joe Louis' biographer and secretary, as well as an award-winning West Coast journalist best known as an enterprising racketeering and court reporter.

It is all too easy to overlook the fact that Washington got his start at his hometown paper, *The Pittsburgh Courier,* as the crusading paper's sports columnist and editor. Washington was among the best known of his generation's black sportswriters, and arguably made the most progress, from the time he started in the mid–1920s to his departure for the West Coast in 1948.

His work of the late 1920s, when he shared the sports beat with William Nunn, Sr., has the innocent, almost cheerleading style common to sportswriting of the day. But by the mid to late 1930s, his work displays maturity, depth and a palpable sense of outrage that star Pittsburghers like Satchel Paige and Josh Gibson were not in the majors where they belonged.

In the late 1930s, Washington and Wendell Smith formed the best one-two punch of any sportswriting team in the black press. Ironically, as Washington's style matured, he actually wrote less; Smith became sports

Chester Washington (photo courtesy Douglas Washington).

editor in 1940, about the same time that Washington moved over to the news desk as managing editor, leaving less time to write the column he called "Sez Ches."

One of Washington's great stylistic advantages was a healthy sense of humor. "His disposition was like sunshine on a cloudy day," wrote Brad Pye, Jr., in a *Los Angeles Sentinel* obituary in 1983, when Washington died at the age of 81. "His writing was just as sunny."

"Balmy breezes crept stealthy up the side and over into the massive concrete sport bowl," Washington wrote in 1930 of a Negro league game at Yankee Stadium. "[Meanwhile], a mighty mass of Harlem's sport lovers—thousands of attractive women in softly-tinted flimsy summer garments and nattily-clad men topped off by vari-colored berets—watched the titanic diamond struggles."

But Washington could also be serious. "When Joe Louis beat Max Schmeling," he once wrote, "he laid a rose on Abe Lincoln's grave." About race relations in America, he wrote simply: "It takes both black and white keys of a piano to play 'The Star-Spangled Banner.'"

It didn't hurt that Washington's beat included the legendary Homestead Grays and the Crawfords, making Pittsburgh for a time the capital of black baseball. *The Courier* itself had a circulation at the time of close to 300,000, the largest of any black paper in the country, and enjoyed a large readership throughout the South.

The newspaper's editor, Robert L. Vann, was an idol to the young Washington, growing up in Pittsburgh, according to a short biography supplied by Washington's son Douglas, the community affairs director at the Wave Newspaper Group. It was to Vann's alma mater, Virginia Union University in Richmond, that Washington headed for college "with high hopes in my heart and $30 in my pocket," as he put it.

It was also around then that Washington established his reputation as a manual typist without peer. He won the Virginia state typing championship and thereafter took a job as an evening typing teacher at Armstrong High School in Richmond to earn tuition money.

Washington also became a self-confessed library-rat in college and read everything he could on writing, speaking and editing. He was eventually appointed college press agent and editor-in-chief of the college annual. "Somehow, Vann got a copy, and wired me to give me a job in his *Courier* editorial department after graduation," Washington recalled years later.

In his "Wave" biography, Washington wrote that he and his wife Alma and two sons moved to the West Coast in 1948 because by then the rest of his family had moved there. "When I received news that my beloved mother had only a short time to live, I quickly decided, like Horace Greeley, to go West."

In 1966, Washington became a publisher, after securing funds to buy two small Los Angeles–based weekly papers, *The Central News* and *The Southwest News*. Five years later, he bought the Hicks-Deal chain of Wave Newspapers, which brought in five more papers and made him a wealthy man. Today the company is still family owned and has eight weekly Los Angeles area papers, stretching from Culver City and Inglewood in the north to Compton in the south. The papers' combined circulation is more than 200,000.

In his biography, Washington listed his hobbies as "golf, golf and golf," and it seems fitting that he became the only black sportswriter of his generation to have a golf course named in his honor. The Chester Washington Course, also known as the Western Golf Course, is south of El Segundo Boulevard in Los Angeles and hosts a number of local and regional tournaments.

Washington's numerous journalism awards include an honorary doctorate from his alma mater, Virginia Union University; Publisher of the Year from the National Newspaper Publishers' Association; and "Best Editorial of the Year" from the Greater Los Angeles Press Club.

"The past is history and the present is a challenge that we have to accept," Washington once said of his newspaper company. "We are making progress, the community is responding enthusiastically and the future will tell how well the job is done today."

The following columns were originally printed in *The Pittsburgh Courier.*

July 30, 1927

"Y're Out"

Ever think of the Umpire and how he feels,
When your charge him with giving you unfair deals?
Ever wonder what he's thinking when he says "Y're Out!"
And you think you made a safety on a healthy "clout."

Well, he's human and usually does the best he can—
And perfection is not found in either child or man.
Sometimes there's just a shade between the "safe" and "out,"
Then, no one likes to see a man begin to fret and pout.

The secret is to play and play and still to play the game,
If you would earn a niche in Sports Immortal Hall of Fame,
And if one's "called" against you, and there's a little doubt—
Be man enough to take it and let it be an "out."

Don't fuss and fret and moan and cuss and protect in excess.
In life's great Game, such setbacks will help you gain Success.

August 20, 1927

Just off the train and back to the roll-top after a whirlwind trip to New York, this "indefatigable 'Knight of the Pen'"—nowadays the typewriter—grabs the dutiful, old reliable Royal that in response seem willingly and rapidly to pound out line after line in a joyous story of how:

"The Grays Captured Manhattan"

The words, "The Grays," will be scrolled;
The players' names will be enrolled—
Written in letters of polished gold,

And often the story will be told—
Of how they knocked the Giants cold!

Homestead Gray stock soared "sky-high" Sunday when the Pittsburgh club, not only raided the value three points by three victories over the Lincoln Giants in Smoketown, but invaded the very meat of the "market" itself, and incidentally the spacious abode of the Giants' Protectory Oval, and snatched an 8–6 triumph together with the heart of the fans present.

Literally, the Homesteaders "bearded the lion in his den," with Lefty Williams playing the "hero" role. The big Gray "Smokey" cloud swept over fair Manhattan, swooped down upon the Giants like a typhoon and whisked away the New York–Pittsburgh series just as mighty whirlwind would do. Old Man Pluvius ruled the second game of a scheduled doubleheader after a drizzle turned into a downpour.

Lovers of baseball got plenty of thrills during the Giants-Grays tilts and both outfits showed up well. Diamond stars of national reputation showed their wares before an interested public and everyone "got their money's worth." And who couldn't enjoy seeing Manager Lloyd, Rojo, Joe Williams, Washington and the rest of the boys perform?

Games of the caliber that have been just staged will always be looked forward to expectantly by followers of the sport the country over!

April 6, 1930

"Oscar an Asset at First"

When the 1930 edition of the Homestead Grays departed for Hot Springs, Arkansas, to go into spring training, local fans were much concerned about the first base problem and speculation was rife as to who would fill the gap left open when "Jap" Washington was left behind. Thus the news that Oscar Charleston is cavorting around the initial sack in masterful style and batting like a demon besides, is extremely gratifying to the many friends of the Homesteaders in this district.

Charleston first functioned as a first-sacker back in the halcyon days of the late C.L. Taylor's famed Indianapolis A.B.C.'s. There Oscar's uncanny judgement as an infielder and his unusual talent as a batter won him innumerable friends and showed his wares in the diamonds of the Orient where he was labeled as the peer of all outfielders. Charleston's brilliant fielding in the outer gardens and his heavy stick work for Hilldale during the past few seasons helped to keep the Derbyites always near the top.

In addition to being an able player, Charleston is one of the most popular players in the game. He was to Philadelphians what Smoky Joe Williams was to the New Yorkers when the latter was with the Lincoln Giants—their hero. Scores of school kids turned out regularly just to see Oscar perform. He was to them what Babe Ruth is to kids of a lighter hue.

Charleston's homers, triples, doubles and singles broke up many an old ballgame last season down in the old park where Clare Darbie used to hold forth, and fans here are waiting expectantly to see the mighty Oscar scintillate on local diamonds.

June 1, 1935

"Watching the Cubans— Craws Open in New York"

Broadcasting from directly behind home plate in the press box of beautiful Dyckman Oval, surrounded by Dan Parker, *Daily Mirror* sports expert; Romeo Dougherty of *The Amsterdam News;* Bill Clark of *The Age;* and all the lads, we're asking our trusty typewriter to give you all the highlights and the "lowdown" on Gotham's most eventful and colorful opener in a decade...

It is a perfect baseball day... The newly vamped stands and playing field are things of beauty and a joy forever... An overflowing crowd packs the park... Bright new American flags are draped in front of the boxes and pennants flutter leisurely in the gentle early summer zephyrs... His royal baseball highness, Commissioner Ferdinand Q. Morton and the league Chairman W.A. "Gus" Greenlee of Pittsburgh are among the official guests of Alexander Pompez, the man who made his "dream come true" in the erection of this model ballpark... The Crown Prince of Fistiana, *Joe Louis,* our All-American monarch of the knockout art, was the leading celebrity present and it was your correspondent's privilege to introduce him over the "mike." We recalled it was the second time the writer had this opportunity. The last time was in Chicago at the East-West game last fall... He was a Golden Gloves champion then, almost unheralded and unsung. But what a difference today! In nine months, Louis has become the toast of Chicago, the idol of New York and the model fight hero of a nation. And the crowd paid Joe a thunderous ovation... This must seem like celebrity day, for there's John Henry Lewis, that fighting phantom from Phoenix, recent conqueror of Bob Olin, the light-heavyweight champion, and more recently tucked under the managerial wings of "Gus"

Greenlee, walking beside Joe Louis as he leads the parade of players and notables to the flagpole. It's tough trying to "keep up" with the clan of Louis...

The National Anthem is played as a massive American flag is raided heavenward and a respectful silence settles over the stands... We spotted the handsome gray-haired head of Frank Sutton, newly appointed dietician for the Joe Louis camp at Pompton Lakes, New Jersey.... And there's "Highpockets" Hudspeth's head (a former Lincoln Giant first base sensation) towering above the crowd like a fog over "Frisco"... Two nattily dressed teams, the New York Cubans in spotless white uniforms with crimson monograms, and the Homesteaders in blue-gray uniforms with the word "Grays" in navy blue... Bernard Deutsch, president of New York's Board of Aldermen tossed the first ball across the plate, and the opening game was on... The hard-hitting Homestead Grays, socking the ball with a vengeance all afternoon, won both encounters from the Cubans, copping the first tile 12–3 and grabbing the second portion of the doubleheader by a 6–3 count.

July 17, 1935

PRESS BOX, LEAGUE PARK, CLEVELAND, OH. — Apparently inspired by the presence of Jesse Owens, the Pittsburgh Crawfords and the Chicago American Giants tried to made the Ohio State Streak feel at home here today by showing flashes of track and field meet tactics as the Craws ran amuck with their legs and bats to win both frames of a doubleheader by scores of 17–2 and 12–8.

We wondered what Owens, the bounding Buckeye Bullet was thinking about as he sat sandwiched between his mother, his bride, three sisters and a brother, marking up the runs, hits and errors on a scorecard as such flashing bolts of baseball flesh as "Cool Papa" Bell, Marshall, Crutchfield, Willie Wells, Bankhead, Josh Gibson and Chet Williams thundered by his box bound for first base. Between games, we asked him how Bell's speed compared with other runners he had seen. We recalled Cool Papa's bullet-like dash to first to beat out a perfectly laid-down bunt to third. "He's just about the fastest ballplayer I've ever seen," Jess said. "And I believe he has more speed than Ben Chapman, the Yanks' outfielder." This was a perfect tribute to the clean cut Crawford centerfielder, who had the amazing record of a triple, a double, four singles, two walks and one "flied out to left" in nine trips to the plate, scored six runs and had a couple of stolen bases thrown in for good measure in the two games.

The popular Jesse also came in for a well-deserved compliment from Hizzoner, the Mayor of Cleveland, in person, who called Owens "the fastest human on two feet." It was prior to the presentation of a basket of flowers to Ohio State's streamline sprinter and one to Lem Williams, Cleveland's promoter of the Craw-Chi. batting carnival. Mayor Harry L. Davis said that it was an honor to pay tribute to such a splendid young fellow as Owens, and that the citizens of Cleveland held him in high esteem, both as an athlete and as a man. Davis also predicted that Owens would bring honor to the United States, Ohio, Cleveland, himself and his race in the Olympic Games in Berlin next year.

We buttonholed His Honor in his box a few minutes later and he confided to us: "He's a great kid, and we're going to put him to work for us [the city] next week in the athletic and recreation department. We believe that he will be a great inspiration to the boys as well as a splendid teacher of physical fitness and sports."

And now to the games, which thrilled nearly 8,000 fans, who turned out to pay honor to Cleveland's comet and watch the two catch Negro National League clubs in action. The engaging thing about the two games was the remarkable hitting ability of the stellar players on both clubs. The first game was still in its infancy, in the second inning to be exact, when our own Josh Gibson of the Craws drove a mighty wallop 15 feet beyond the 405-foot mark in left field for a homer, with two men on the basepaths. That was only the beginning. The Crawford bats began to resound with the regularity of a machine gun, and before the smoke had cleared away and the game was over, the Pittsburghers had connected for a total of 14 hits to score 17 runs to their rivals' two. And all the while, the Crawford and Chicago base runners and ball hawks scooted around the infield and outergarden like a bunch of frightened greyhounds, while several of my Nordic press associates up in the reporters' perch marveled at their speed and daring.

Chicago tried hard to break up the Crawford's batting picnic in the second game, but bedlam broke loose again in the first and third innings of the second clash and the Craw lumbermen hammered out another 12–8 victory.

March 7, 1936

"Jim Nasium," writing in the current issue of "Liberty" bemoans the fact that baseball today lacks the color that the game thrived on in the stormy diamond days of yesteryear.

Admitting that some of the "fight" and glamour is gone, there is still lots of color in the great American pastime. Writers like "Jim" and major league owners may not know it, but many of the players on the leading colored clubs have it and plenty of *it*. Not only in the shading of their skin, but in the brilliant and dazzling brand of baseball they play, they are more colorful than the leaves of autumn.

"Who Could Be More Colorful Than..."

• Satchel Paige... The sky-scraping, shuffling speedball pitcher with his windmill winding and sinewy throwing limb that reaches out like the long arm of the law. Then he shoots one down the batter's bridled path. Out on the West Coast where the winter season is just closing, they're comparing the shuffling Satchel to the great Christy Mathewson of "fade-away" fame. And some say he rates with the mighty Rube Waddell. He seems to specialize in making "fan" exponents out of the major leaguers. The "suitcase" wizard fanned Gus Suhr of the Pittsburgh Pirates three times and continuously shot his fast ones safely by such noted big-league swingers as Ernie Lombardi, Johnny Vergez and Harry Lavagetto. And early yesterday, he saw a testimonial in a New York tabloid by the Yankee recruit Joe DiMaggio, who says that Paige is the best pitcher he ever faced. Joe, who has faced the cream of the crop, further testifies: "Satch has a curve with so many bends, it looks like a wiggle in a cyclone; it gave optical indigestion. And his fast ball? Say, when he fires it, the catcher gets nothing but ashes!" Such color and popularity must be served.

• Josh Gibson... The big, hard-hitting young Pittsburgh Crawfords' home run sensation, who is reputed to have made the longest hit ever recorded in Yankee Stadium. Josh makes a cut at the ball as healthy as the beloved Babe Ruth himself, and his four-base clout record for 1935 ran up into three figures.

• "Mule" Suttles... Spectacular first baseman of the Chicago Giants, who is also one of the mightiest fence busters in colored baseball.

• Raymond Brown... Fast, young and fearless catcher of the Homestead Grays, who is also a splendid outfielder, a sure hitter and a daring player.

• Willie Wells... The flashy shortstop of the Chicago Giants who has one of the surest throwing arms in baseball and a consistent hitter.

• Buck Leonard... The far-reaching, brilliant portside first baseman of the Homestead Grays, who is one of best and most sparkling initial first sackers in the game.

• "Fats" Jenkins... The human jackrabbit who speeds around the outfield for the Brooklyn-Newark club like Ralph Metcalfe and Jesse Owens. He's rated as one of the surest flycatchers of the business.

• Young... Brainy and colorful catcher of the Kansas City Monarchs, who behind and at the plate and at bat is a rare performer.

• "Cool Papa" Bell... Colt-like and bespectacled outfielder of the Pittsburgh Crawfords, who covers more territory than the state of Texas. He is also one of the fastest men in baseball on the basepaths.

• "Turkey" Stearns... Chicago's hard-clouting contactman at the plate and dependable centerfielder, and one of the most spectacular performers in the game.

• West... The stellar first baseman of Tom Wilson's Nashville club, who is one of the greatest all-round players in the business.

• Vic Harris... Pony outfielder of the Homestead Grays, who is always a threat at the plate and one of the most valuable and steady players in colored baseball.

• Oscar Charleston... The Old Maestro of Swat, who is liable to knock a homer after taking two strikes and (finish) up any ballgame. Oscar is still a great first baseman and one of the best field generals the Pittsburgh Crawfords or any other club ever had.

• "Showboat" Thomas... A "show" in himself, or on anybody's ball field is this scintillating first sacker for the New York Cubans. He scoops 'em out of the dirt like a spade and pivots like a man on the flying trapeze.

• Jake Stevens... The diminutive Rabbit Maranville of colored baseball and stellar shortstop of the Philadelphia Stars, who shoots 'em across to first like a bullet, he is one of the greatest fielding first basemen of modern times.

• Jud Wilson... Mighty man of swat of Philadelphia and nicknamed "Hack" and Lon Chaney, who is a terrific batter and a brilliant and colorful addition to any club's infield.

• Slim Jones... Elongated schoolboy pitching sensation of Ed Bolden's Philly Stars, whose curves and slants made New York sportswriters ask scores of questions. They also rated him as one of the best curveball pitchers they had ever seen.

• Martin Dihigo of the New York Cubans... Big, powerful and versatile... A great hitter and a brilliant utilityman, who, only last week, held the Cincinnati Reds of the National League to three hits and beat them in an exhibition game in Puerto Rico.

And many others...

National Negro League contests, the East-West game and the New York four-team doubleheaders have been as full of color as the rainbow hues of a Christmas necktie. And they will retain their color and glamour for many seasons to come.

One of these days, some courageous big-league owner will be broad minded, resourceful and far sighted enough to realize that the infection of some stellar Negro players will add the *color* that the majors need, and our boys will be given the chance they deserve.

And who knows, but that colored players may give to big-league baseball a stimulant similar to that which the Joe Louis influence have professional boxing.

Pleading our support in a campaign against "closed doors" in the major leagues, I remain,

Your constant correspondent,
Ches

May 9, 1936

"Satchel's Back in Town"

Like Lulu, Satchel's back in town!

The long, lean Leroy "Satchel" Paige, prodigal son of the Pittsburgh Crawfords, who shoots a baseball across the plate like an expert machine-gunner, is glad to be back "home." The stellar Satchel must have missed his admiring "rabble" and the "boys" out in the wilds of Bismarck, North Dakota last year, so he's back to sparkle in the National Association firmament.

Like Joe Louis and Jesse Owens, Paige is another one of those stars who fell in Alabama. Little Leroy was born in a modest farm in Mobile, Alabama, not far from the Brown Bomber's birthplace, on the night of August 26, 1907. He grew up like a weed in a marsh. When he came to age, he scraped the skies at 6'3". His reach is like the long arm of the law. The satchel-like shape of his feet earned him the nickname that he bears today. His first pitching assignment was with the Chattanooga Black Lookouts of the Southern League in 1925, where his speed gave him a running start toward a spectacular career. Later, he joined the Birmingham Black Barons, where his ability gained him national recognition.

Last year, we jumped on Satchel with both feet and advocated his exile from the National Association when he treated his two-year contract like a "scrap of paper" and walked out on the Crawfords. We contended that he was setting a bad precedent for the league. And we have no apologies to make for our stand. But now, he's back in the fold again, and we're going to chronicle his praises as one of the greatest speedball pitchers in the game today.

"Satch" holds the distinction of being one of the hardest players in the game to handle, but also the unique honor of being Negro League baseball's biggest gate and name attraction. He is to colored baseball what

Dizzy Dean is to the majors, with many debates developing as to which player is the "dizzier" at times.

But Paige has many virtues. In addition to being a brilliant pitcher, he has "that certain thing" that the fans like. Whether it's "it" or "that" or maybe "that's *it*," we're not sure, but whatever he has, the pasteboard purchasers go for it in a big way. On the diamond, Satchel "outsteps" Stepin' Fetchit on the screen. He's a natural showman as spectacular as a circus and as colorful as a rainbow. Added to this, an amusing nonchalance marks his every move even under the most trying circumstances.

It was a crucial moment in the East-West game of 1934 when two-picked all-star teams were vying for national honors. There's a man on second, no outs, and no score. A signal from the East's manager and a tall, shuffling shadow moves slowly from the dugout toward the pitcher's box. He ambles along slowly, like a pallbearer in a funeral procession. "It's Satchel Paige," the crowd roars. "It won't be long now," someone in the stands echoed. And it wasn't . . . after Satchel got ready to pitch. He picked up a handful of dirt . . . rubbed the ball . . . glanced in differently at third . . . looked sidewise at the catcher for a signal . . . shook his head up and down slowly . . . wound up like a man cranking a "Model T Ford," and then finally let one go. It shot across the middle of the plate like a bullet and the batter apparently never saw it. Three men faced Satchel in that memorable inning, and three men walked back to the dugout while the scorekeeper chalked up three "S.O.s." The crowd roared its approval . . . and Satchel's team won the game, 1–0.

Pitching against the Dayton Ducks only a few days ago, the Satchel diamond circus wheeled into action again.

As if to prove that one of the overanxious Duck batters was "all wet" about his idea that he could get a hit, Satchel yelled to catcher Josh Gibson:

"What one of y'all you [calling for] now, Josh?"

Gibson dropped two fingers below his mitt.

"Well, there you are," Satch called, as he shot it across the plate.

The bewildered batter reached in vain like a man reaching for the moon and the ball whizzed by.

"How'd you like that?" the sweet Satch smiled.

Again the crowd roared, and, of course, the Crawfords won.

Among Satchel's many achievements include the decisive defeat of several teams composed of major league stars, striking out 18 in one game and completely shutting out the Homestead Grays for the first time in their history.

The return of Satchel to the Crawfords will greatly enhance the drawing power of this already popular club. And Owner Gus Greenlee says Satch is worth every penny he's spent on him. Especially in the east, fans are practically Crawford crazy, and when Satch sweeps into town with them, it will be like the coming of the circus. Already, New York is waiting with keen expectancy the triumphant return of that elongated, streamlined pitching sensation who beat out Slim Jones of Philly in 1934 in the Yankee Stadium game. And Satch is also anxious to show his wares again in Gotham this Sunday when the Pittsburgh Crawfords appear there in their league opener with Alexander Pompez's New York Cubans.

With Paige back in the league, he may practically be the Moses who will help to lead Negro baseball into the promised land of economic prosperity. At any rate, when Satchel comes to town, watch the turnstiles click.

April 24, 1937

With baseball in the air and the trend of most sports' talk turning to the grand old game, we cornered Umpire Johnnie Craig, one of the most respected sepia strike-callers of the National Association, and asked him to take the stand.

Having witnessed thousands of major league games, in addition to handling some of the most important games in the history of Negro baseball, we believe that Craig would be able to bring out some unusual angles about the great American pastime. His testimony speaks for itself:

Q. What is your full name?

A. Johnnie L. Craig.

Q. How long have you been working as an umpire in big-time baseball?

A. Nearly 10 years.

Q. What inspired you to be an arbiter?

A. First, my interest in baseball generally, and, secondly, my admiration of the work of three big-league umpires, Bill Klem, along with Stark and Quigley.

Q. What particular feature about the work of these umpires impressed you?

A. Well, Klem of the National League was always firm in his decisions and always the master of every situation. I got most of my inspiration from him. Then, I liked Stark for his alertness and Quigley for his neatness and precision.

Q. Did you ever get a chance to meet and talk with these major league umps?

A. Yes, I met them all, and even got an appointment to talk with Klem in 1935 at Ebbets Field, Brooklyn.

Q. Tell us something about the meeting?

A. Well, Klem took me out in the stands near the first base line, and told me to watch each umpire closely. He then showed me the proper stance for base umpiring and also explained how to work behind the plate to keep a clear line of vision on the ball.

Q. When and where did you handle your first game?

A. At Forbes Field for the Homestead Grays in 1928. The umpire scheduled to work didn't show up and Cum Posey, the Grays' owner, gave me a chance to work.

Q. How did you feel in that game?

A. I felt all right. I was handling the bases and it didn't seem very difficult.

Q. When was your biggest thrill?

A. When I worked for the first time behind the plate. It was another involving the Grays, out in Braddock, Pennsylvania. I'll never forget it. Vic Harris was the first man to come to bat, and I give him credit for establishing my confidence.

Q. How did that happen?

A. Well, I believe I called the first ball badly, and instead of condemning me, Vic encouraged me. That meant a great deal to me.

Q. Where were you on the afternoon of July 4, 1935?

A. At Greenlee Field, handling that memorable game between the Crawfords and the Grays.

Q. We recall that Satchel Paige pitched no-hit, no-run ball to blank the Grays that day. Do you remember any other unusual feature about that game?

A. Well, Satchel's pitching was great, but another remarkable thing to me about the game was Dula's wonderful twirling for the Grays. He, too, turned in a great pitching exhibition until he wrenched his arm near the latter part of the game and had to be removed. It was a great contest between two great moundsmen.

Q. In your opinion, what sepia pitcher has the fastest ball?

A. Satchel Paige.

Q. Whom do you rank second to Satch?

A. Leon Day of Newark's Eagles.

Q. What twirler seems to have the widest-breaking curveball?

A. Harry Kincannon, formerly of the Crawfords, now with the Grays.

Q. Which pitcher has the best drop in Negro baseball?

A. Schoolboy Johnny Taylor of the New York Cubans.

Q. Among the catchers, who do you consider as "tops" in all-around ability?

A. Bizz Mackey of the Nashville-Washington Elites.

Q. Who do you consider the most accurate thrower?

A. Josh Gibson of the Grays.

Q. Where do you rank Pepper Bassett of the Craws?

A. A great prospect and second to Gibson.

Q. Did you ever see him pull his rocking chair throwing act?

A. No, but I hope to be calling 'em when he does.

Q. What player do you rank as the greatest you ever saw?

A. Oscar Charleston.

Q. Name the three best outfielders today.

A. Fats Jenkins, Bankhead and Vic Harris.

Q. What pitcher of last season do you consider as the best prospect?

A. Griffin of Washington.

Q. Who is the toughest man to handle in baseball?

A. Jud Wilson, if his teammates back him up in his contention. But, it's just because Jud has a fighting heart. He's an ideal competitor and never lets up while he's playing, but he's a hard man when he has a contention.

Q. Do you think Wilson will make good as manager of the Philadelphia Stars?

A. If he can instill the Wilson spirit of hustling into the other Philly Star players, they will have a great team.

Q. What do you think of the trade that gave Josh Gibson to the Grays and Pepper Bassett to the Crawfords?

A. I think it will benefit both clubs.

Q. Since you've seen hundreds of big-league games in addition to countless games between colored clubs, how do the best sepia players compare with the best in the big-leagues?

A. The best in our leagues have just as much ability as the major league stars. The only thing our boys lack is opportunity.

Q. Name a few of the players who rank right up there with the big leaguers.

A. Satchel Paige, who would have ranked along with Walter Johnson, if given a chance in the majors; Matlock, McDonald, Holland and Jud Wilson appear to have everything it takes.

Q. What one thing do you think will do more than any other favor to help Negro baseball?

A. To enforce stricter discipline among the players. It will make the performers respect the league and the fans more, and thus help colored baseball to go places.

April 12, 1941

"Grays' Baseball Skies Aren't So Blue Because Jolting Joshua Is Missing"

The Grays have the "blues"!

Just when baseball's "blue skies" and springtime's sun have started chasing away the grayish clouds, and the horizon is taking on a rosier hue, the Grays are showing symptoms of a bad case of the "blues."

And it's all because Jolting Josh Gibson, the hardest hitter in baseball and probably the greatest Brown Bambino of Swat of all times, won't be wearing the gray-tinted garb of the famous Homesteaders this season.

Lured by lucrative offers from Mexico, the big brown Belting Beauty of Negro baseball disregarded his current contract with the gallivantin' Grays and hired himself away to play down in the lands of wide sombreros and dark-skinned dancing damsels.

And, as a result, the Grays' management, believing that the loss of Josh will mean a shortage of about $100,000 in income for the 1941 season, have filed suit for breach of contract to recover that amount.

Looking on the situation from a seat in the pressbox, it is not for us to decide as to who is right and who isn't. The matter has been placed squarely in the hands of the court. We can, however, point out that both parties in the legal proceedings have some grounds for their action.

JOSH WAS THE GREATEST DRAWING CARD
IN THE ENTIRE SEPIA LEAGUE CIRCUITS

Justly advertised and ballyhooed as the greatest home-run hitter in the game, it is obvious that Gibson was the biggest drawing card on the Homesteaders' roster. A four-base hitter who had banged the ball farther than Babe Ruth in Yankee Stadium and set new long distance hitting records in several major league ballparks, it was only natural that the "fence bustin'" Josh was a super "come-on-in-er" at the box office.

And with the name attractions who stood up in the glorious records of the Grays of years gone by, such as Smoky Joe Williams, Oscar Owens, Lefty Williams, Jap Washington, Oscar Charleston, Satchel Paige and the colorful catcher Perkins, the bleacher-jarring Joshua remained as one of the Grays' most important aces in the hole.

Not that Gibson's loss will mean that the Grays won't have a good ballclub. (They sopped up three titles since 1934 and have been good for a decade.) Because scrappy manager Vic Harris, with pitchers Ray Brown and Edsel Walker & Co., the brilliant Buck Leonard at first, Carlyle at second, Easterling at third and "Jelly" Jackson at short, Benjamin in center, Whatley in right and Vic himself in left, believes that he still has the best-balanced and the most formidable club in Negro baseball.

Still, the Grays are justified in their contention that the loss of Gibson will have a devastating effect on the gate receipts.

GIBSON WAS INFLUENCED TO GO
BY BIGGER FINANCIAL OFFERS

On the other hand, Gibson is probably "jumping" to Mexico for the same reason he went to Puerto Rico for the winter of 1939 and to Venezuela in 1940. It is reported that Josh received $700 a month for six months, plus transportation and all living expenses for himself and his wife while in Venezuela.

And it has been reported that his salary down in baseball-crazy Mexico is just around the $800 monthly figure, which is more than sepia league clubs can afford to pay their players.

Satchel Paige succumbed to the same lucrative lure and was barred from organized sepia baseball because of these practices. And other players have been guilty of "jumping" around like Mexican jumping beans.

The Grays contend that Gibson, under an agreement dated January 27, pledged himself to report to duty with the Grays on April 1.

It is now up to the court to decide. And usually, judges frown on anyone—and even a ballplayer—who disdainfully regards a contract as "just a scrap of paper."

May 30, 1942

"An Open Letter to Judge Landis"

Judge Kenesaw M. Landis
Commissioner of Organized Baseball
Chicago, Ill.

Dear Judge:

Big-league baseball should take a tip from the U.S. Navy. The navy barred colored men from general service in ships, limiting them to "below-the-deck" duties as messmen.

The majors keep colored players off their rosters, allowing only a few to perform as assistant trainers.

But the navy was big enough to catch the spirit of the times. It was broad enough to realize the trend toward democracy in practice as well as in word, in all of our American institutions. So it dropped some of the bars . . . and Secretary Knox of the navy announced a change of policy. And from now on, our boys who are qualified will be enlisted for service on all types of ships up to and including destroyers.

The navy, like organized baseball, is steeped in tradition. But it was big enough to sense the swing toward liberalism and to make a timely, real American beau geste.

Maybe the major league moguls will tell you that the induction of Negroes into their ranks would create a training problem. The navy faced that issue too. But they didn't let it stump them. They answered it by establishing a training base for the new recruits at the Great Lakes Naval Training Station. So couldn't your owners answer their problem by establishing a "farm" team of colored players to be groomed for eventual use into the big leagues? At least that would be a step in the right direction.

And maybe the owners are giving you the alibi that their managers and players don't want colored stars on their rosters. Our own sports editor, Wendell Smith, exploded that theory in a comprehensive poll of National League managers and players, who, almost without exception, declared that they wouldn't object to sepia stars who could make the grade.

Then possibly, they are contending that the colored performers couldn't measure up. But there's a fellow named Josh Gibson, the bronzed Bambino of Swat, who is knocking balls over big league park fences regularly and could blast that theory into oblivion in one afternoon and bring back memories of Babe Ruth and Lou Gehrig in their halcyon days. And if you don't believe us, ask Jimmy Cannon of the *New York News,* who has been crusading for an opportunity for colored players in the big leagues for a long time, because he believes that they have the stuff of which major league players are made.

Then, there's that alibi about the housing of players in the deep South and other points. Our own George Asten, assistant trainer of the Pittsburgh Pirates for over 20 years, can answer that one. He solves his own problem every training session, even in the deep South, with little difficulty.

Then, the owners might ask what contribution colored players could make to the big leagues. In the first place, they would certainly make the game more colorful. Providence endowed them with that attribute. Then, our top-notch players are super showmen. Take Satchel Paige and Josh Gibson, each one a "super-super" attraction. Moreover, some of our sepia stars could certainly plug up the big gaps being left in many of the teams made by the draft boards.

Finally, the use of Negro stars would help at the gate . . . an important point to be considered. If an aggregation of sepia stars can draw about 50,000 fans every year at the East-West game, certainly a game with a group of colored stars, mixed into an inter-racial contest, would draw more. Dorrie Miller got his big chance to man a navy gun and won the Navy Cross. His heroism at Pearl Harbor was not in vain. And, if Jolting Josh Gibson, the batting Big Bertha of Negro baseball, were only given an opportunity, he could be one of the big guns of major league baseball. And no country or organization should deny a chance to make good.

Sincerely,
"Ches" Washington

P.S. Did you read about the Kansas City Monarchs drawing 30,000 in Chicago last Sunday against Dizzy Dean's major-league all stars and beating the stars 3–1?

DR. W. ROLLO WILSON

The Red Smith of His Day

It could be said that Dr. W. Rollo Wilson died as he wanted—at a ballpark, after covering a sporting event. Death came to the erudite *Philadelphia Tribune* and *Pittsburgh Courier* sportswriter in 1956 at the age of 65 outside Connie Mack Stadium in Philadelphia as he left a Philadelphia Eagles–Pittsburgh Steelers football game.

"Maybe it was ironic that Rollo died like he lived, covering the world he loved best," wrote Bill Nunn, Jr., in *The Courier,* the week after his death. "It's possible, of course, that Rollo might be alive today if the urge to get back on the job wasn't a part of the vigorous vitality that made him the dean of [black] sportswriters."

Like Frank Young, Wilson wore round granny glasses that gave him a scholarly air, and, also like Young, he was an institution of black sportswriting with a career that spanned upwards of a half century. Wilson's column had many names, but it was usually called "Through the Eyes of W. Rollo Wilson."

Wilson's work was well-respected; it had style, humor and a poet's touch. "And eat!" he wrote about the dining habits of a young Josh Gibson. "That boy has a keener zest for food than does your fat correspondent."

Wilson was a moderate among the black sportswriters of his day. While others hammered away at the injustices of a segregated game, Wilson generally steered clear of black-white controversies, reserving his more potent criticism for internal matters involving Negro league players, officials and promoters.

He could still be tough. A 1945 *Tribune* column on Satchel Paige, for instance, admonished the star pitcher for arrogance, but put it all in the past. As Wilson wrote, "The snob is a regular fellow now."

Wilson just may have been the purest baseball writer of his generation. Like Red Smith, his work was folksy with a certain playfulness. Both men got away with it because of the overall superiority of their writing. Indeed, occasional Wilson columns were directed to "Sol," his longtime friend Solomon White, a first baseman with the Philadelphia Giants, who, in 1907, published the *History of Coloured Baseball*, the first definitive source on the black leagues.

Even his farewell column, written in 1945 for *The Tribune* as he went into semi-retirement, is a study in moderation. "'Thirty' in press parlance means the end; that there isn't any more," he wrote. "And so I come to the end of my last column in *The Tribune* for a little while at least. It's been pleasant working here.

"I have been identified with sports too long that this is the end of a column which began in 1914," he continued. "I choose to call it a sabbatical, an auf Wiedersehen instead of good-bye."

Rollo Wilson (portrait by Steve Spencer).

Wilson took some unusual sabbaticals during his long career on the sports pages. In 1934, he served as commissioner of the Negro National League. In the 1920s, he was an inspector and later deputy commissioner for the Pennsylvania State Athletic Commission. At other times, he was a fight manager and promoter.

Indeed, while serving as the Eastern correspondent for *The Courier*, he also worked in Pittsburgh, and later, as a chemist for the city of Philadelphia. After leaving *The Courier* in the 1930s, he wrote first for *The Philadelphia American,* and later, in the 1940s, for *The Tribune.*

Sports were his passion. He was present at all of the events of the era, and his staples included Philadelphia-area baseball, Joe Louis fights and the Penn Relays. *The Amsterdam News* called him the "far-famed . . . most brilliant sport[s] writer of color in America" in a 1926 story boosting Wilson as Pennsylvania boxing commissioner. The story added that he was a "right royal good fellow." Wilson was a native of Franklin, Pennsylvania, where he worked for two years as a reporter for the local white newspaper, *The Franklin Evening News.* He was a high honors graduate of both Temple University, and, in 1914, the University of Pittsburgh School of Pharmacy. During World War I, he served in the Medical Corps at Newport News, Virginia.

Unfortunately, other biographical details of Wilson's career are lost to history. He became a widower at a relatively early age, and blended a steady flow of friends with a touch of whimsy. "[He drives] a red Buick, which, we are told will make its next appearance in more subdued colors [as it] dart[s] through Philadelphia's narrow streets," *The Amsterdam News* reported in the story touting him as boxing commissioner. Alas, we'll never know whether Wilson ever changed the colors on that Buick.

Of the following stories, those dated 1930 and earlier were first printed in *The Pittsburgh Courier;* those dated 1944 and 1945 were written for *The Philadelphia Tribune.*

July 14, 1923

"Eastern Snapshots"

James Stephens' Philadelphia Giants are finding New England cities very much to their liking. Danny McClellan has his team moving like a steamroller, flattening everything before it. To date, the outfit has won 14, lost one and tied one. They expect to be on the road until late in August.

Manager Alex Pompez and his Cuban Giants are general favorites throughout the East. The genial Cuban has several stars under him, and the only thing that keeps men like Baro, Chacon, Fernandez and Oscar out of the big leagues is their color. Oscar can make a baseball do everything but talk.

Baseball in Philadelphia is not the paying proposition this year that a lot of managers hoped for, generally speaking. The only way the big white teams can make it is by scheduling the more prominent colored teams. The sorry showing of the Lincoln Giants, Brooklyn Royals and Baltimore Black Sox in the Eastern League has affected their drawing power with P.B.A. teams.

To stimulate interest in the P.B.A., a championship series is now being played, although none of the colored team are participating. "Romeo and Juliet" minus Romeo.

If Solomon were living and attending Hilldale ball games, he would add another to the four things that he confessed he could not understand, and that is the strange hostility that many fans exhibit towards Louis Santop. Fortunately, they are small in number, though loud in voice.

Santop is generally considered by those who know baseball to be the greatest Negro catcher in the game, despite his 30-odd years and 215 pounds. Ask any white fan who is the greatest drawing card on the Darby team. Ask him who is the most feared batter in the P.B.A. The answer will always be Santop. "Top" has that rare thing—baseball brains. He thinks too fast sometimes for some teammates, and if the later fails to go with the play, it makes the big fellow look bad in the eyes of the average fans.

The "average" fan last year made a bum out of young Catcher Richardson by swelling his head with their demands that he supplant San-top. Happily, Hilldale Manager Bizz Mackey has too much sense to follow the trail of that young Texan.

Next to Hilldale, the best drawing colored team in the Philadelphia District is the Washington Potomacs. This team's access to popularity is one of the wonders of the season. Two men started with nothing and from that nothing have evolved a high-class baseball unit. Manager Ben Taylor has developed an organization that play the snappy, intelligent game that the fans demand.

Secretary E.J. Butler, who gave up his business in Indianapolis to follow Manager Ben into the sport field, is one of the reasons why the Potomacs are going big. His shrewd handling of the business end of the club, his affable disposition and courteous treatment of players, fans and competitors have been factors whose worth none can estimate.

June 17, 1924

Some folks say that umpires are not of the same species as you and me. However, we know better. Don't they make plenty of mistakes? And, years ago, we were told that "to err is human." Speaking of umpires, we do not know any class of citizenry that should travel more than these arbiters of the diamond. It would broaden their outlook and teach them something of the brotherhood of men. If they stay on one ball lot too long, they stagnate and their vision becomes warped. We have in mind an official in the Two-Team League (Franklin and Oil City, Pennsylvania) a few years since. In his first—and last—game, he could not call an Oil City "Oiler" out; he never saw his pitcher hurl the ball. Everything was "safe" and "strike" as far as they were concerned. Had there not been another ump in the game, the battle would have endured till the crack o' doom. After the game, a committee of prominent Franklin men escorted the judge to his hotel, wrote out his resignation for him, paid his hotel bill and accompanied him to the "moonlight" express for Pittsburgh. They advised him to travel, and, for all we know, he is still on his way.

October 9, 1926

"Why, Snickers," Dobby Hicks asks, "shouldn't this be a hard year on champions? Isn't '26 two thirteens?" And, of course, he's right that far. Thirteen world's champs and who knows how many national and local champs have joined the big parade to oblivion. The most recent upset was the Monarch Giants of the Negro National League. In their playoff series with Rube Foster's Chicago, they needed but one game out of three to win, and so confident were the powers that be that they could turn the trick, that all World Series advertising was put out with Kansas City named as the opponents for the Bacharach Giants, winners in the Eastern League. What happened? The Chicago boys swept the three games and before the Monarchs knew what it was all about, they were on their way East to engage the Bees.

I have sat in on many stirring scenes, but that game at the Shore last Friday was as thrilling as any I have witnessed during a fairly active life as a spectator of things athletic. Currie and Henderson are two of the best hurlers anywhere and had something on every pitched ball. Each uses his head for other than a parking place for his hat. The support accorded each in the pinches was high class.

The Rube (Foster) has what in ear days we called "the will to win." When he was with Hilldale, he used to loaf around the Colyumn's West Philly headquarters. What did he talk about? Nothing but *baseball*! Each night, he would live over the game of the afternoon before, dissecting it from the first putout to the last. Truly, he is a man who loves his job, and he is never happy unless he is playing or talking the game. He is a credit to his profession.

Rat Henderson was in trouble all the way, but the Rat never pitches his best except when such conditions obtain. Time after time, he crossed the Western batters and *never* gave them a good ball to hit.

I still claim that the B-Giants have the best all-around infield in colored baseball. Little Garcia rose to the heights on Friday when he saved Henderson's game for him by phenomenal stops and throws in the sixth and the ninth innings. When the test came, Cummings and Lundy and Marcelle never faltered. Their defensive play is a thing of beauty and a joy forever.

When Chaney White scored from first on Lundy's single, he made Jelly Gardner look foolish. Jelly retrieved the ball and ran toward the infield with it. What he was thinking about, if anything, nobody will never know. White, with the tying run, speeded up to third base and took the chance. Gardner, flustered by such effrontery, hurried his throw and lost his man. Hereafter, this Western star will take no liberties with the elusive Mr. White.

Mayor Ed Bader of the Shore resort, enjoyed every minute of the game, and he is a keen and analytical student of all sports. Here is an example of his knowledge: Frank Young of *The Chicago Defender* remarked that Sam Thompson was leading the league in batting, whereupon the Mayor asked why, if he was the league premier, should he be hitting in the number two hole, instead of clean-up or fourth.

Big Boy Jones had the time of his life. There was his golden chance to show his stuff, and strut it he did. The Bees' famous announcer displayed a satorical ensemble that amazed and delighted the crowd. His vintage flannels were of a '96 model and the rest of the costume graded up to as recent a date as 1920. He refused to commit himself as to the origin of the big green ribbon that adorned his megaphone.

June 25, 1927

Some of these days, I'll see a greater and more versatile ballplayer than the Cuban Stars' Martin Dihigo, and when I do, I'll write, wire or phone the details to each reader of this Colyum, collect. I thought that Bird was better at first base than anywhere else. Then I saw him pitch and changed my mind, seeing in him the class of the league on the mound. And since then, I have reversed by opinion numerous times. Saturday, he worked in the shortfield and Senor Chacon should be glad that Dihigo is all-around athlete, else he would have no job waiting for him when he ceases to ride his charley-horse.

I have not witnessed a better team in action this season than Alexander Pompez's outfit. With a pitcher on first base, a first baseman at short and a hurler in the garden, they still looked the part of potential champions. Try such a combination on your club and see what happens. The Cubans were good last year, but they are a whole lot better now. Pedrosa and Caldenez have been dropped and Alfonso, once with Molina in the west, has been put on second base. Crespo has moved over to third. Dihigo is supposed to be the regular first-sacker, though it does not seem possible to keep the big fellow there. Portuondo, now a casual, is second-string catcher and infield utility.

This trip of the Islanders has been a very profitable one for the percentage column, and when they return home on Saturday, they should play before one of the greatest crowds ever assembled in Davids Stadium, Newark. They will play the West New York semi-pros, a local white team. On Sunday, the Harrisburg Giants will be the attraction, and it's just possible that this conductor will find it necessary to be in North Jersey at that time. The following Sunday, July 3, the Paterson Silk Sox will leave their park to battle at the Stadium. This is the first time in history that this team has played away from home on Sunday, if you want to know how important the game is!

One instinctively likes this Senor Pompez. He impresses you with his sincerity and his evident love of baseball. It took him a long time to get a home yard, but now that he has one, he aims to show the rest of the magnates how to conduct such an institution. Here is a man who has been the victim of some of the most atrocious umpiring ever meted out. Has he told his arbiters to give the other clubs the works? He has not! They have been advised that they must not be "homies," that his visitors must be given an even break all the time and that plays must be called as they see them. He wants no favors because he believes in winning ball games by the ability of his men alone. He is a real sportsman and one could exhaust his vocabulary and praise him no more highly.

April 6, 1930

A picture comes to the desk from Cum Posey in Hot Springs, Arkansas. It is the 1930 edition of the Homestead Grays. In the group are 13 players and the two club owners, Posey and Walker. One or two of the faces are new to me, but the rest of the boys are ones I know. While they have barnstormed with the Homestead outfit, some of them are appearing as regulars for the first time. Of these, the most important are Oscar Charleston and Judy Johnson.

I consider Judy Johnson one of the most valuable men in Negro baseball, and by all odds, the best third baseman. And Judy, let it be known, did not reach that point in my esteem, over night. His has been a long, hard and brilliant climb. I remember when he first broke in with Clan Darbie and Bill Francis trying to make a shortstop out of him. (Will was the regular third sacker himself.) The following year, John Henry Lloyd was at the Hilldale helm and he shifted Johnson to third base, told him that was where he belonged, and he has been on the hot corner ever since. Each season, he has improved in batting, fielding, base-running and diamond knowledge. On the field, he is a winning player who never quits fighting; off the field, he is a gentleman and a credit to the game. You can always depend on Judy being in condition to give his manager his best services, and that should mean a whole lot, but apparently, it did not in the past. I don't think Johnson was ever fully appreciated by either the Darby owners or fans. In spite of the fact that his salary requests had not been granted, he was the outstanding athlete on the Hilldale payroll in 1929, and had the best season of his career. He made more hits than any player in the American Negro League, and established other offensive and defensive marks. He surpassed the great Marcelle—who had been the leading sundown third baseman—in every respect, and came into his own. And as I salute him, I bespeak him a still greater record.

Of Oscar Charleston, much has been written. I doubt if the game has ever produced a great player and again I am reminded of his appearance at Forbes Field, home of the Pittsburgh Pirates. He flashed so much skill and brilliance against Rube Foster's American Giants in that memorable series between the Chicago club and C.I. Taylor's A.M.C.'s of Indianapolis that the writers on the daily dope sheets went crazy. Some of them openly declared that he was a greater star than the Pirates' Max Carey, then at the height of his days. They said he batted like a Cobb and fielded like a Speaker, and there could be no greater praise in that era.

In 1929, Oscar was troubled with a sore arm and this handicapped his throwing and hitting, but still he was able to maul the apple around .400. I believe it is Posey's intention to use him on first base to round out what should be the greatest infield in Negro sport.

With Charleston, Scales, Stevens and Johnson in the first line, the Grays have nothing to fear. Scales was the best second baseman last season down east. He has it in him to rate that way again. Jake Stevens is a natural ballhawk and was ever the toast of followers of the Clan. I believe that his wanderlust is dead and that he will stay "put" for the season. Buck Ewing is a better catcher than most of the others hereabouts.

The Gray outfield and pitching staff looks none too good, and I expect changes in both. I don't look for the blonde and truthful Master Ross, Joe Williams and Lefty Williams to be able to carry the burden. Sandy and Cum have listed George Britt and Oscar Owens as catcher and outfielder respectively. The former Baltimore utility man is a good hurler and a better catcher, but he has perhaps reached the stage in his career where he gives his best services only when his activities are confined to one position.

A few nights ago, I shook hands with Dennis Graham in Pennsylvania Station, Pittsburgh, as the "misses" and I dashed for a Philadelphia train. I didn't have time to mention baseball to him, but I'm betting he will be back in a Gray uniform before the season is many weeks old.

The boys told a story about Graham, one which has never reached print, and his reaction to that automobile crash of the team last summer. It was up in the Pennsylvania mountains, and it was See Posey's car that skidded off that bump-backed road near Lewistown. As the men crawled from the wreckage, other cars stopped to render assistance. Graham crept painfully out of the sedan, and from the ditch, straightened up and made a halting path to the door of a farm house. To the lone woman who was standing there trembling, he asked brokingly: "Lady, have you got a mirror?"

"Why, yes," came her wondering reply, "but what do you want with a mirror, now of all times?"

"Well, I want to see my face and see if it is cut," was the surprising comeback of the sturdy Grays' outfielder.

June 14, 1930

The lamentable attendance at baseball games played by sundown teams in the east proves that this writer has no selfish motive when he insists that the public will not patronize the game unless the teams are in a league. And this is not meant as a merry ha-ha at the predicament in which the owners find themselves. All of them deserve a better break than they are getting. Not over 300 people were on hand last Friday night to see Hilldale and the Lincoln Giants in a twilight game in Philly. And you can guess what is happening in Baltimore when I tell you that George Rossiter is forsaking the Westport park next Sunday to meet the Lincolns in New York! That does not argue well for the attendance in the Monumental City.

The public wants to know that competition means something and the players, too, want to feel that a victory is something more than "just another ball game." They want their hits compared with their fellows in the batting averages of the league. They want to read what the figures say about the pitching and the fielding. The fans want to prove their contentions by the records. Just the other night, I heard this age-old argument, "Judy Johnson woulda got that ball." And then, "I know Marcelle woulda got it, but Judy woulda messed it up just like that fella did." And then the battle was on!

Sport thrives in organized competition and it is a safe bet that there will be some sort of league in 1931, or that most of the present owners will be out of the game.

September 27, 1930

Young Jake Stevens (for he *is* young, even if he has been a top shortstop for nearly 10 years) is sold on Joshua Gibson, the fast and clever kid catcher of the Homestead Grays. I saw Stevens in Detroit several weeks ago, and after introducing him to me, Jake began to sing his praises. A week or so later, I saw Jake in Philadelphia and once again, the theme of his saga was Joshua Gibson.

I don't believe the tale has been told of how this lad joined the Grays. If I am wrong, if you have heard it before—read it again! As it came to me, the Posey-Walkermen Grays were about to begin a game, and Buck Ewing had split a finger. The manager was at wit's end and for someone to send in as a sub. Up in the grandstand was a young husky on his way home from work in the Edgar Thomson US Steel Mills. He was attired in the garments of his calling, the hallmark of a horny-handed son of toil.

"What ho" cried he, when the rumor that the great Buck Ewing was hors de battle ran through the sweltering crowd. "Give me his jerkin and his weskit, his armor, and I'll catch the fireballs of even the aged Joe Williams."

He lumbered down on the field, hobnailed shoes and all, and offered himself a living sacrifice to old Cum Posey. Since nothing better could be done, Posey accepted his services.

"And mind yuh," snarled Cumberland, whose English shows no evidence of the classic education he obtained while playing basketball at Penn State, Pitt and Holy Ghost College (now Duquense U.), "if yuh can't ketch, don't bother to turn in Buck's suit; jes keep a 'goin!"

Well, the kid could catch and did catch and is still catching. He's green yet, but the ripening process is moving apace. He has not mastered the technique in throwing to second base, but he kills off all the fast boys who try to steal. His stance at the plate is worse than Pimp Young's, but he gets his base hits. His motto is "a homer a day will boost my pay."

And strong! Ask any ballplayer about what a rough playmate Oscar Charleston is. Then ask any Gray athlete how this gawky kid mishandled the Hoosier Hustler at Forbes Field a pair of fortnights back. Cum's young partner, Charlie Walker, calls him "Samson."

And eat! That boy has a keener zest for food than does your fat correspondent. He spends more money for "snacks" than any of the other players lavish on three meals. It takes a tremendous amount of fodder to satisfy his growing body and nourish his 194 pounds of bone and muscle.

And curious! Gibson is continually asking questions, and for that reason, they gave him the truthful and blond Master Ross for a "roomie." Ross is ready with an answer for any sort of question. His store of information is exhaustive, if not always accurate. Master Ross defends himself in this fashion: "If you ask a question, you don't know the answer. Therefore, if my reply is sometimes at fault, what difference can it make since you do not know that I am wrong?"

They should have named him "Josher" instead of Joshua, for he sure can kid the kidders. For confirmation of this, you may communicate with the renowned Raleigh Mackey, now laboring for the Baltimore Black Sox. On a recent Sunday in the Monumental City, the kid so worked on the perspiring Bizz each time he came to bat, that he was fit to be tied, as the expression goes.

"Aha!" sneered Gibson, when Mackey clumped out to the plate, "so, this is Mr. Mackey, the famous catcher and batter. I've been readin' a lot about you in the papers. I believe you were in the games in Pittsburgh

Friday and yesterday. You didn't do so well, did you? Well, you're gonna do worse today.

"Oh, you missed that one! Too bad. Now sir, here is one right down the alley. What! Only a foul? My fault, sir. I forgot that I had called for one on the inside. Don't hit at this one, it's an off ball. So sorry! The darn fool pitcher crossed you up. His control was bad and he cut the corner. Yes, Mr. Mackey, that was three strikes. You are excused for the time being. Perhaps you will do better the next time; you may hit it to the infield."

Daltie Cooper was telling Otto Briggs that Willie Foster of the American Giants is the greatest pitcher he ever saw.

"Huh," cracked Gibson, "the reason Cooper says that is because Willie Foster struck *him* out!"

February 26, 1944

Once again, "taps" sound for a sportsman, a former soldier and a long-time friend. Once again, the column bids farewell to another who was pictured here more times than once in another decade.

Charlie Tyler died violently in his Avenel, New Jersey roadhouse a few days ago, the victim of a crazed gunman whom police still seek at this writing.

In recent years, he was a member of the Asbury Park trap shooting group—the Sycamore Gun Club—and helped to make it one of the powerful units of the Eastern Skeet and Trap Shooting Association, whose guns are silent for the duration. Congenial, hospitable and a skilled shooter, he was genuinely liked in all of his social and business connections. His tavern was a rendezvous for sportsmen and socialites of the eastern seaboard.

But Charlie Tyler was all of those things and something else to me. He was a symbol, an example of what happens to colored businessmen who enters Negro baseball with the cards stacked against them by the inner council. And this is Charlie's story fashioned so that even those who run may read:

Years ago, when Gus Greenlee was trying to put the game on a paying basis and was willing to gamble his tens of thousands to do it, he thought of Charlie Tyler and Newark, New Jersey. The two had soldiered together in the World War, and both had come home to reap financial success of a sort. Well, Charlie agreed to go along, and with the late Henry Williams, they placed a team in the Jersey town. The next year—1934—Gus got his league functioning and Newark was a member.

Then, as now, club owners believed that an all-league schedule was impossible and that games must be played several days a week with independent clubs. A club owner just did not write to other owners and suggest dates in his park. It was not that simple. What you did was to turn your club's billing over to a booking agent and he took care of your open dates for you. Of course, there was, and is, a mere matter of a 10 percent cut for him for his efforts.

The city of Philadelphia was a pot of gold for all ball clubs in 1934, and some of you ball fans recall that Greenlee's Pittsburgh Crawfords practically lived here that year. They had a constant booking with all of the major clubs of the section. So too did the Grays and the Nashville Elite Giants. And what about Tyler and his high-priced Newark club? Were they sharing in the prosperity?

He was getting North Jersey booking that his organization dug up, and it was none too rich. Around the Quaker City, he was getting practically nothing. Why, you ask? Well, that is what Charlie asked the booking agent, and Tyler told me that he was advised that "there are too many colored clubs and I cannot take care of you very often."

That cured Charlie Tyler of his yen for baseball. He could not live on the crumbs that fell from the booking agent's table. Like Jim Stevens and George Robinson and Ike Washington before him, he knew that he was trapped. He realized he was only throwing money down a rathole with never a chance to get it back. He finished out the season, sold his franchise to Abe Manley for the proverbial song and got out.

And that is Charlie's baseball biography—brief, bitter and bald. In later years, as other associations brought us together, sometimes we talked of that experience, and whenever we did, it usually ended on his rueful, "Well, I got away from them with my shirt, anyhow."

May 10, 1944

The unfortunate circumstances surrounding Josh Gibson, star catcher of the Homestead Grays, have now become public property due to his being held at Gallinger Hospital, Washington, D.C., for observation.

There are some who have been telling me that Gibson's domestic life was stormy and that one or two former nervous breakdowns were due to this fact. Several times this spring, word had reached me that Josh was a sick man, and officials and players of the Grays have often tried to persuade him to return to his home in Pittsburgh and put himself under medical care. He refused each time. It is said that recently, he had become a heavy drinker and that this habit was aggravating his mental condition, making confusion more confounded.

Gibson had been suspended by President Jackson of the Grays in Baltimore about two weeks ago for breaking club rules about drinking, and had to be removed from Bugle Field. After the game, "Sunnyman"

Jackson ordered Josh to return to Pittsburgh, but he declined to do so, going to Washington instead.

A few days later, he was arrested for disorderly conduct, and a brief examination at the station house led to his being taken to the hospital.

Philadelphia fans will remember a night at Shibe Park back in 1942 when the Grays and Kansas City Monarchs were playing their World Series, and how Gibson collapsed in the dugout and a doctor had to be summoned from the stands. Later on, he went to Hot Springs to rest and recuperate. It is reported that he spent some weeks in a Pittsburgh institution last summer at the club's insistence.

The passing of likable Josh from the baseball picture will leave a void not easily filled. He came to the Pittsburgh Crawfords in 1928. The Crawfords were then a playground team, and the late Roy Sparrow tried to convert him into a third baseman although Josh insisted he was a catcher. Eventually, he had his way. He was snatched from the budding Greenlee empire in 1930 by Cum Posey, and ere the end of the season, his terrific hitting had won for him national recognition. In the years that followed—back to the Crawfords and then again with the Grays and in Mexico—Josh was bracketed above such great catchers as Bruce Petway, Frank Duncan, Louis Santop, Bizz Mackey, Larry Brown, John Beckwith, George Britt, Rojo, etc. Big league players praised him, and Walter Johnson once said that his "selling price" in the big leagues would be at least $200,000.

Hardly into his early 30s, Gibson's career will have ended too soon. Baseball fans everywhere are hoping and praying that he will recover his health and be in there again, beating 'em to all corners of the lots.

May 16, 1945

Among the master showmen of all time in the world of sports is this Satchel Paige (whose baptismal name "Leroy" is almost lost in the pages of the past) and his visits here are almost as certain as Republican victories in city elections. And, so local fans will be on hand Monday at Shibe Park to welcome a guy who once was as unpredictable as June 1945 weather.

It's been many a season since Paige first strolled out on the Hilldale diamond to oppose Clan Darbie. He was with Frank Warfield's Black Sox, of Baltimore, and was not so well known then. Followers of class sports pages had read about him with the Birmingham club, but he had not yet proved himself in the big towns of the East. A pair of seasons later, he was with the Pittsburgh Crawfords and his reputation for ability and eccentricity was made. In addition to having a crack ball club, Gus Greenlee had the best "press" any team ever enjoyed. The Big Fellah spent thousands of dollars a year keeping the Crawfords in the newspapers and Satchel was fruitful copy of team secretary John Clark.

Well, "Satch" believed a lot of the things that were written about him and became a prima donna. He had his own car and used it to journey from city to city, ceasing to ride in the team bus. Time and again, he was pinched for fast driving. He would refuse to don a uniform except on the days he was slated to pitch. And he forgot some of those, failing to arrive at the park to take his turn on the mound. And these and other stunts did the morale of the club a lot of no good. But when he did pitch, he was one of the best that ever did it. His fastball became a legend. In off-season barnstorming games, he gave big-leaguers the same treatment he used on race batters. Finally, the zing was gone from the fastball, and Paige fell on parlous days.

Finally—I think—Satchel called himself into conference and went over the books. He found out what was wrong in his business and took steps to remedy the condition. Some of the frills and furbelows were dropped from his attire, figuratively speaking, and for several years, we have had a vastly different Satchel Paige. To his pitching equipment, he added a brain that he had refused to use in the days when he could cannon-ball every pitch past the most dangerous hitters. He retained the on-duty color and sloughed off the off-duty trimmings. Now, he travels with his fellows, in uniform every day and is on the field for all pre-game activities. The snob is now a regular fellow. This is the Satchel Paige who will be on the Shibeshire hill against the Boldenmen on Monday night for Wilkinson's Kansas City Monarchs.

The Monarchs have added Jackie Robinson, All-American football star from the University of California at Los Angeles, to their infield, and he was one of the three players given an alleged tryout by the Boston Red Sox in the early spring. Manager Frank Duncan, who was himself a K.C. institution and still an active player, says that in a year more, Jackie will make the older Missouri fans forget that a gent named Jose Mendez ever played the shortfield there. Add to them all of the old favorites including outfielder Brown who has hit a home run in every game he has played in Shibe Park and you have the usual colorful Kaysee Monarchs, year after year one of the top outfits of sundown baseball.

DAN BURLEY

The Most Versatile Black Journalist of His Generation

Dan Burley's lengthy 1962 obituary in *The Amsterdam News* details his varied career as a much-traveled newspaper reporter and editor, musician, lexicographer and author. Only in the third-to-last paragraph does it even mention his brief but able career as a sportswriter.

Burley, who was eight days shy of his fifty-fifth birthday when he died of a heart attack, reported on sports for perhaps a half dozen years. Indeed, he just may have been the most versatile black journalist of his generation. Like Chester Washington, he was better known for other things.

"A confidante of the great and the small, the good and the bad, the rich and the poor, Dan was probably the best known [black] journalist in the U.S.," *Ebony* reported in a 1963 tribute to Burley.

Burley learned his trade the traditional way, working from the time he left Chicago's Wendell Phillips High School as an editor for *The Amsterdam News, The Chicago Defender, The New York Age, Ebony* and *Jet.* At the time of his death, he was publishing his own newspaper, *The Owl.*

Burley was perhaps best known for his editorship from 1936 to 1948 of *The Amsterdam News,* for which he also covered sports and wrote a popular entertainment column, "Back Door Stuff." It was through that column that Burley became known, according to *The News,* as "almost an institution" in the unusual annals of black American lexicography. His specialty was the language of the streets, which he picked up in his reporting. Burley published several volumes that detailed his findings, including *The Original Handbook of Harlem Jive,* an analysis of 1940s style "hep" talk, the preferred shorthand way of talking among musicians.

He was also instrumental in establishing the famous *Amsterdam News* Midnight Shows at the Apollo Theater on 125th Street in Harlem. The shows became annual affairs and drew entertainers from throughout the music and dance world.

Dan Burley (portrait by Steve Spencer).

Burley himself was a talented play-by-ear pianist and songwriter whose jazzy, ragtime satirical compositions include titles like "Pig Foot Sonata" and "The Chicken Shack Shuffle." He was also acknowledged as the inventor of "riffling," a tinkling, suggestive piano style especially suited to the Depression-era house rent parties that were prevalent in Harlem in that era.

Burley was born in Lexington, Kentucky, and raised mostly in Fort Worth, Texas. His father was a slave turned Baptist evangelist, while his mother taught at Tuskegee Institute in Alabama under Booker T. Washington.

Although his career as a sports journalist was brief, Burley made his mark, mixing his stylish column with solid baseball sense and a historian's understanding of the significance of Jackie Robinson's arrival in the major leagues. To Robinson Burley devoted some of his best reporting. "Robin-

son and Roy Campanella have the trail cleared ahead of them," Burley
wrote in 1948, a year after integration. "Both can hit as well as play their
positions with great versatility. Both are team players, a rare combination
of talents, and in addition, they occupy the singular role of Negroes sparking the morals of white players."

No wonder *The Amsterdam News* saw fit to write of Burley that he
"quickened his reporting and commentary with his own special brand of
wit and often sharp insight into [blacks] as people and their society as a
tragi-comic brand of American Folkways."

The following pieces originally appeared in *The Amsterdam News.*

May 16, 1942

"This Is About Our Boy, James (Soldier Boy) Semler"

Looking like a man with not a care in the world, the astute Mr. James
(Soldier Boy) Semler, owner of the New York Black Yankees, swung
around the corner from Seventh Avenue into 125th Street, his lips pursed
as he whistled a popular tune. Now, quite a few of the "boys" know Mr.
James (Soldier Boy) Semler and Mr. James (Soldier Boy) Semler knows
quite a few of the boys. So we won't argue about that. Instead, we turn our
attention to Mr. Semler's peace of mind, his prosperous appearance and
his philosophical view of the immediate future.

You see, Mr. James (Soldier Boy) Semler is a baseball man and has
been for umpteen years, although we would hesitate to mention the actual
period of years because Mr. James (Soldier Boy) Semler might interpret
it as meddling with his age and think we were doing the wrong thing—
especially right through here when a gentleman of his standing would
profit all the more by being mistaken for a much younger man.

We were talking to a friend at the "Doughnut Hole" as 125th Street
and Seventh Avenue, where most of us with frugal purses nigh unto pay
day are often wont to gather to bemoan extravagances that forced us to
such an extreme.

Naturally, there was a great scrambling and pushing and shoving on
the part of the gentry in the "Doughnut Hole" to get near Mr. James
(Soldier Boy) Semler, to feel the soft texture of the smooth camel hair coat
he sported, to admire the handkerchief in the upper pocket of his jacket,
and to envy the sharpness of the man and to ask him with bated breath how
he could whistle so merrily when we were at the ultimate extreme—the
"Doughnut Hole."

It so developed that we were able to learn that Mr. Semler had just blown into Harlem from parts West and South, mostly the latter, where he had been for more than a month or so observing his 1942 edition of the New York Black Yankees in action and trying to forget the fable told at the Negro National League meeting last winter in Baltimore.

It was remarked, in that instance, that the Dodgers had sold somebody to the Reds for $25,000. The wag at the N.N.L. pow-wow came up with the snide observation that one of the better known Negro ballclubs had traded a player who hit 67 home runs in 1941 to another team for a smoked Virginia ham, a bird dog and a couple of auto tires.

Now, such a remark should rightly be considered the highest in blasphemy and should automatically condemn the narrator to durance vile. Since the narrator got away in the uproar of laughter and shouts of indignation, there is nothing to be done about it, but let it die, if it will.

The return of Mr. James (Soldier Boy) Semler, as in the past umpteen years, officially announces that the Black Yankees are to play baseball at home next Sunday.

And the return of Mr. Semler also speaks loudly of the fact that another season of Negro baseball is to be inaugurated this Sabbath at Yankee Stadium. At the same time, the return of Mr. Semler, attired as fashionably as he was and plentifully supplied with his own cigarettes makes it emphatic that something is in the wind.

It took very little deduction to find out that Mr. Semler's cheerful whistling was over the fact that his 1942 Black Yankees stack up on paper as the pennant winners in their league and the potential big money-making nine of the year.

Those close to the portly pilot of the Black Yankees can agree with this column that in other years, Mr. Semler hasn't looked so happy. In fact, there was apparently a great falling of the flesh about the jowls and a haunted look in the eyes and a nervous twitch to the fingers as they reached for your cigarette pack in those days of trials and tribulations for Mr. James (Soldier Boy) Semler as he prepared to launch his club on another season.

In those days, it is recalled, Mr. Semler talked glowingly and encouragingly just before the mid-winter league meetings about what he would do next year. After the meetings, he would lapse into a more dour state from which he seldom emerged during the playing season when his club put up such dismal exhibitions that its most rabid supporters cheered in whispered outbursts.

In those days, the popular conception of sports decorum was to feel sorry for James (Soldier Boy) Semler and to join in a chorus of abuse to the other club owners who banded together in dark, foreboding conclaves from which came other woes for the Black Yankees.

Thus, James (Soldier Boy) Semler was mostly seen in the role of an

unwelcome stepchild who had to be kept around because he would someday inherit a valuable estate, in this case, finally cash in on his baby, the
New York Black Yankees.

Now, it seems that Mr. Semler's traditional worries are at an end. All
he has to watch is the long arm of Uncle Sam and the guy in the box office.
He's got the team. He's got the backing. He's got the crowd with him. He's
riding the wave.

Allen Johnson, the fabulously wealthy strawberry grower of Mounds,
Illinois, who owns the St. Louis Stars of the Negro American League, saw
Semler's plight and also noted the potentialities of owning a franchise in
New York City.

Where "angels feared to tread," Johnson stepped in with his money,
his Three Ring Circus of Baseball Phenoms, his prestige and his friendship
and the net result: Mr. James (Soldier Boy) Semler swinging around the
corner from Seventh Avenue into 125th Street, with his lips pursed as he
whistled a popular tune.

It is obviously true that no sportswriter in New York has yet viewed
the 1942 Black Yankees so strenuously put through the paces this spring
by the tobacco-chewing, irascible, foxy Tex Burnett. But, this writer has
seen most of the men listed on the roster in action and can truthfully say
that it is the greatest assemblage of diamond material to be found outside
the big leagues.

Take a look at this pitching staff: Chip McAllister, Eugene (No Hit)
Smith, Lefty Calhoun, Charley Boone and Tom Parker, all St. Louis
Stars; along with the veterans, John (Neck) Stanley and Bob Evans. Now
add to that total, Bob Griffin, ex–Elite hurler. They are seven talented
hurlers.

And an infield like this: Chili Mayweather, the home run king, on first
base; Dick Seay, double play sparkplug at second; Jimmie Ford at short;
and Harry Williams on third. Then, look at this outfield—Dan Wilson,
Chin Green, Buddie Armour and Buck Bennett. Behind the plate? Well,
Johnny Hayes and Ray Taylor ought to round out that department. And
round it out in style. Whistle on, Jim Semler. We're whistling too.

August 15, 1942

"Purely Baseball and Satchel Paige"

Leroy "Satchel" Paige, elongated one man pitching show of Negro
baseball, came out last week with a statement that threw a definite
monkey-wrench into the campaign to force the major leagues to stop

discriminating against colored ballplayers because of their race and color. Paige, who has been used as one of the main reasons why Negro talent should be displayed in the big leagues, jumped the fence at Albany, New York, last Thursday when he told newspapermen that any major league club wanting his services would have to offer him at least $37,000 because he earned that amount in 1941. Paige, it was reported, frankly believes Negro players cannot successfully fit into the big league set-up because of the race prejudice angle. The Kansas City Monarchs' luminary declared:

"You might as well be honest about it. There would be plenty of problems, not only in the South, where the colored boys wouldn't be able to stay and travel with the teams in spring training, but in the North, where they couldn't stay or eat with them in many places. All the nice statements in the world from both sides aren't going to knock out Jim Crow."

Paige, it seems, believes that instead of major league clubs signing a few Negro players as it now seems possible, an all–Negro club could be operated in one or both of the major circuits.

I don't blame Paige for setting such a premium on his services. He is in an enviable position: both white and colored ballplayers would like to earn half of what he says he picked up last year. However, Paige is a bit garrulous as those who know him attest. In running his mouth about the program to get Negroes—his fellow playmates in baseball—their long-denied and long-deserved opportunity, threatens to tear down all that has taken newspapers and other public-spirited groups and individuals years to build. In other words, it has been a long road leading up to the present when public pressure can and has forced major league club owners to make public statements. They have been silent all along, refusing to come out of their shells and state why they are against Negroes playing in the big show and on their teams.

Starting with Judge Landis, several of the team, including William J. Benswanger of the Pirates, Gerry Nugent of the Phils, Ed Barrow of the Yankees, Larry MacPhail of the Dodgers and Clark Griffith of the Senators, have gone on record with preliminary statements as to how they feel about the entire matter.

The long road traveled by those fighting for a renaissance in baseball has had little aid and support from the fellows for whom the fight is being waged.

Negro players and Negro club owners, both of whom would be primarily concerned in any renunciation of the Jim Crow line in baseball, have been strangely reticent on the question right along.

For Paige, at his phase of the battle, to open his trap and give the opposite side ammunition doesn't jell so nicely in my icebox.

If Paige, who can still go a few seasons more and on the big time at that, feel that the "problems" involved are too much to consider, why hasn't he pointed that out before? Or last year? Or the year before?

If traveling with teams in spring training and eating and staying with the teams in the North is such a problem today, then Paige certainly should have hollered about it when he was around giving interviews of what he could do in the big show.

However, Paige will find that his latest squawk won't deter those who are committed to the fight to open the door of opportunity to all players, no matter what their color.

The line is down, and even if it doesn't come this year, the big moment for Negro ballplayers is bound to roll around soon.

Public opinion is pressing the question, and under such pressure, the big league owners, the recalcitrant colored players who don't want to believe those Negro sportswriters who have queer ideas about the matter, are bound to give ground.

September 9, 1944

"Chicken-Feed Pay for Negro Umpires"

What about our Negro baseball umpires? They are cussed, discussed, made the subject of all sorts of fuss. They are reviled and often as not, riled as they go about their highly sensitive calling of calling 'em right, knowing that the fans in the stands are prejudicing them from the start, and that the players are the greatest umpire "riders" in the business. If an umpire isn't good, he is subject to spoil an entire game. He can throw players off-key by the way he calls the play, he can incur for himself bitter animosities that follow him off the diamond into his social life. All together, the life of the Negro umpire isn't cheese and cherries by any means.

But when an umpire has to take the burdens of the baseball world on his back and then doesn't get enough pay for an honest day's work to pay his rent, buy food and other necessities of life, then something should be done about it, not alone by baseball officials, but by the fans who follow the game and want to see Negro baseball advance. That's why the letter printed here from big Fred McCrary, a familiar figure at Yankee Stadium games and rated as one of the best arbiters in baseball, black or white, is so pertinent to the issue and filled with factual slants on a deplorable situation.

"Dear Dan," writes McCrary from Philadelphia, "I have often wanted to talk to you, but it seems that every time I have the chance, you are busy or I am leaving town for some other point... I notice your writings in your paper that I read every week about different things that go on in the Negro National League, all of which are true. I have also been reading about what you have to say about the player situation and that is true as well. We, as umpires, never get anything or any consideration from the league; we only go on and work on a basis of "dog, take what we give you." For one thing, I have worked in all the East-West games for the past six years, and up until the last two years, they have only given us umpires $10 to work and three days' expense money. It takes three days to get out of Chicago and to come back. For any other days, we get nothing.

"I have argued with the league owners for more money, or at least for $50, and they, or at least some of the owners, have gone so far as to say that the umpires are not important in a ballgame, and not nearly as important as the players. I know that is not true, because the umpires can make the game what it is, good or bad. I was asked by Moore of Birmingham after the game Monday in Chicago and by Blueitt and the two western umpires to go with them to the room where the western club owners were checking up on their share of the receipts and to see what they were getting for their work. They got $100 and expenses, and Moore's expenses were $35. Dr. J.B. Martin, president of the Negro American League, gave him $135. I saw this with my own eyes.

"I have worked for this league and for the benefit of all owners, and after that, I get no credit. I have gone so far as to rent rooms in different towns where I have had a three or a four game series to work, and they charge you $3 or $4 for a room now, take it or leave it. That is despite getting only $3.50 expense in any one town for three days, which only pays for my room for one night. I pay the difference of the two nights out of my own pocket. I also have to feed myself for the three days.

"Now Cum Posey, secretary for the Negro National League, who gives me this lousy $3.50, sent that expense slip to Mrs. Effa Manley, the league treasurer, to be charged to me. I have gotten $6 and $8 for expenses from some clubs when I was on the road, and they sent that in to be charged against me. I was down in Virginia with the Black Yankees and the Homestead Grays and Posey gave me money to eat and sleep, and he also sent that in against me.

"They pay my railroad fare, and if I would come back to Philadelphia every day or night after the games and go back to those towns the next day, it would cost them twice the money for train fare than it would to give me adequate expense money I pay out of my own pocket. But I help them and that's what I get.

"I wish you would write something in the umpire's favor. You can quote me because what I am saying is true... Yours in sports—Fred D. McCrary.

"P.S. From now on, I am returning to Philadelphia every day, so I'll let them spend that money to send me back. They also voted at the league meeting to give me expense money for the road.—F.D.M."

In the 1947 East-West Classic at Comiskey Park, where a crowd of 50,000—47,000 of whom paid to get in the annual affair—the Negro National League expense sheet showed $62.76 for the transportation of two umpires, $20 for their expenses, and $15 each for salary. The players got only $50 a man. This year, the players went on strike and refused to play until a promoter agreed to pay them $200 each. But, the umpires didn't go on strike at all.

With the umpires of such an important affair getting only $15, Dr. J.B. Martin, American League president, and Thomas T. Wilson, president of the Negro National League and owner of the Baltimore Elite Giants, split a cool $3,099.61 between them. That means while Tom and J.B. were eating steaks at Jim Knight's Palm Tavern on Chicago's 47th Street, McCrary and his associate umpires were scuffling in the chili parlor.

Mr. Effa Manley of the Newark Eagles seems to be about the only owner in the N.N.L. who can see the disparity of pay and the treatment of umpires, especially since Negro baseball is having a banner season in gate receipts. It was she who broke up the sorry spectacle of umpires running from club owner to club owner after each game trying to collect their pay, or standing on the sidewalk until late in the night to get their measly salary, while the boys in the back room told tall tales of the days when they were young and otherwise took plenty of time before paying off. Maybe, some day, these things will be straightened out, but only when men like McCrary ask for what is rightfully and morally theirs.

August 4, 1945

"To Rickey, Stoneham, MacPhail: 'Straighten Up and Fly Right!'"

Branch Rickey and the others who set National League policies ought to be ashamed of themselves. They know that their backs are against the wall in the vexing and unwelcome question of whether the Negro ballplayers shall be admitted to big league competition, and, in the manner of the boys on the turf, have been busy laying down a heavy smoke screen to cloak their real intentions of evading the issues at whatever cost.

The year, 1945, will go as significant because of the fact that for the first time, Negro ballplayers were actually tried out by National League clubs. The idea that the National League club that granted these trials to colored ballplayers had no intention of hiring them does not enter the equation. However, progress has been made, and the fact must be pressed relentlessly to achieve an end that seems to be in sight.

While there is much discussion pro and con about the advisability of taking over-age ballplayers like Dave "Showboat" Thomas, the first genius of the New York Cubans and talkative Terris "The Great" McDuffie over to Branch Rickey as the best representatives of Negro baseball, there is no evading the fact that the gate has been crashed.

AND LARRY MacPHAIL KNEW
ALL ABOUT OUR PLAYERS

Those who remember Larry MacPhail when he had the Brooklyn Dodgers will recall that Larry made no pretense of wanting to see Negro ballplayers in a trial attempt for his club. The fiery redhead, now boss of the New York Yankees, plainly stated to a group of us who waited several years ago to see what he would do about giving qualified Negroes a trial with the Dodgers, that he knew the history, background and ability of every Negro player in organized Negro baseball, and consequently did not need to have the trial to see what they could do. He then proceeded to name ballplayers with a familiarity that escapes many of our top Negro sportswriters.

This shows that the National League, through their representatives, agents and various farm clubs, keeps a close check on everything baseball, whether it is played by Chinese, Hindus, Negroes or Czechoslovakians. They are in the business and baseball is their number one consideration. That's why it seems so phony and roundabout for Rickey et al. to stage a series of phony trials, trying to evade the pressure of public opinion, at a time when the issue was undeniably hotter.

JACKIE ROBINSON'S ABILITY WAS QUESTIONED

In case I am making an overstatement in connection with these trials, I perhaps would like to qualify the observation with the remark that the Boston Red Sox possibly didn't know too much about the ability of Jackie Robinson, the former U.C.L.A. halfback wizard who also is a whale of a shortstop and played with the West Coast Institute while in college, but in the case of McDuffie, Thomas, Jethroe and Williams, Rickey and Tom Yawkey probably knew more about them than the Negro League club owners who have them under contract.

The pressure of public opinion plus the passing of liberal laws in various states, particularly New York where the state FEPC poses a formidable barrier to those who seek to continue practicing un–American discrimination against people because of race, creed or color, will act very swiftly to eliminate the conditions that now prevail in organized professional sport, particularly baseball.

It is almost a certainty that none of the major league clubs playing in New York City in 1946 will get by without Negroes in their lineup. Forces are busy right now to take advantage of Gov. Thomas E. Dewey's rather sensational mandate that Jim Crow in employment must be stamped out in New York and are moving slowly but definitely toward marshalling forces for a showdown battle about the issue this winter and next spring.

THINKS NEW YORK CLUBS FIRST TO BE HIT

The New York Giants, the New York Yankees and the Brooklyn Dodgers are the three clubs that will feel the brunt of the onslaught. Persons interested in furthering this fight have let it be known that they intend to grant no quarters in seeing to it that justice is done to the hundreds of qualified, competent Negro ballplayers who are kept out of the big show because their skins are not white.

The position is inexcusable on the part of the club owners. If Rickey, Yawkey and Stoneham were in such towns as Washington, D.C., St. Louis, Atlanta, Birmingham or Chittling Switch, Mississippi, I perhaps would not be inclined to be too hard on them because that location tells the story. But, here they are in the most liberal state in the union, and in the biggest, the most important and the most liberal city in the world, setting themselves up as arbiters of who shall make a living and who shall not and making their conditions and findings on the color of a man's skin.

FEW FANS WILL FORGET
MEMPHIS BILL TERRY OF GIANTS

The prejudiced practices by Stoneham in the Polo Grounds over the years is well known. Few fans will forget the insults Negroes received while Bill Terry was managing the team that played under Coogan's Bluff. When Terry was there, an incident happened that I think will never be forgotten. That was when Terry picked up a small Negro kid with kinky hair, had him on the bench and let the ballplayers, including himself, rub the kid's head for luck in sight of thousands of fans in the grandstands. Such incidents were not uncommon at the ballgrounds. Stoneham and those who operate the Giants have a lot to live down, and to live it down, they should straighten up and fly right on the issue of whether or not Negroes are good enough to play in that park.

Rickey has a great chance of becoming a top liberal along with Hugo Black, now Justice of the United States Supreme Court; Henry A. Wallace, former Vice President and new Secretary of Commerce; and others. He must make up his mind, however, to take the step, even if that step is in defiance of the wishes of such diehard old reprobates as Clark Griffith of the Washington Senators, Sam Breadon of the St. Louis club and others who have yet to see the light. But, he has got to be big, he has got to see the thing in its proper proportion, that is, seeing it in the light of its relationship to real American harmony and goodwill.

The beating-around-the-bush process of rounding up one of two non-descript Negro ballplayers and focusing them in the public spotlight with phoney tryouts and meddling in the affairs of organized Negro baseball will have to be put aside.

Perhaps Rickey will prove to be the man. He seems to be of the caliber to do the right thing once he makes up his mind. Since 1946 augers ill for those who expect to skip by again with anti–Negro practices still in force, Rickey would be wise to get his house straight before the year is out.

In fact, it wouldn't be a bad idea for Rickey to start right now writing his speech for the boys when they gather for the winter meetings. There, he should read the law to them because the handwriting is already on the wall.

August 10, 1946

"The Senors Get in Mrs. Manley's Hair"

Mrs. Effa Manley settled back in her chair in the last row of the grandstand at Yankee Stadium, high above home plate. The fading sun etched fancy patterns across the cool green, upon which her Newark Eagles were locked in mortal combat with Ernie Wright's Cleveland Buckeyes. A goodly crowd was there, estimated after much counting of the fingers, by Frank Forbes, who announced the total attendance out of the corner of his mouth, adding in the next breath that allowances must be made for a reduction of the estimate of 13,000 because he hadn't enough fingers to indicate those venturesome folk who were strolling in the aisles or swarming around the hot dog man.

Down in front sat Abe Manley on the one side and Jim (Soldier Boy) Semler on the other. Terris McDuffie, the stormy petrel of Negro baseball, was in the middle. While no spies could be seen hovering under the seats or sneaking up on the conferees, the report persisted that Manley and Semler were in a verbal duel to the death as to whether McDuffie can be reinstated in the good graces of sundry folk, including Tom Wilson, the N.N.L. prexy, Ed Bolden, Ed Gottlieb, Alexander Pompez and the re-doubtable Pittsburgher, Sunnyman Jackson. You see, McDuffie hid his lanky frame south of the border, down Mexico Way, a season or so ago, in search of more gold, while in righteous wrath, senors Wilson, Bolden, Gottlieb, Semler, Manley, Pompez and Jackson voted to ostracize him from the good graces of Negro organized baseball for five long years. An ardent campaigner for his own cause, McDuffie has been visiting the boys in their offices, intent on "getting this thing straight," so he can make some gold here in the States. Mayhaps he was making headway Sunday, with senors Semler and Manley. Mayhaps not.

Anyhow, returning to Mrs. Manley, she frowns and smiles from afar as she follows the progress of the baseball being played on the Yankee Stadium diamond. From afar, we also noted a swift change in her expression. Her eyes suddenly narrowed, her frame grew taut like a chicken making ready to pounce on a worm, a slow flush of deep anger spread from her neck to the roots of her hair. Up she jumped, and down the aisle she flew, as surprised fans on either side looked apprehensively behind her, sure that somebody must be chasing her for robbing a bank or for putting a firecracker on a streetcar track. Down behind the home plate box seats, she stopped, rushing into a clot of foreign-looking gents gesticulating and talking up a lot of "chili con carne," "tortillas" and "casa manacas" to two of the Newark ballplayers. The ballplayers looked quite a lot like big hefty Johnny Davis, the home run hitting Eagle outfielder; and Lenny Pearson, big, bruising first sacker. Her knowledge of Spanish limited to such words as "chili con carne," "Latino," "Pompez," "Garcia" and "Martinez," Mrs. Manley broke out into a fusillade of good old Newark English, spoken with a brogue usually associated with Brooklynese and Philadelphia Dutch. "What are you going, talking to my ballplayers?" she shrilled as the foreign-looking hombres fell back, abashed. "Davis, you and Pearson are in uniform and playing a game," she said. "You go back to the dugout. I'll see both of you later. Now, you fellows should be ashamed of yourselves, trying to steal my ballplayers right under my eyes. This is awful. I never heard of such a thing. Aren't you ashamed of yourselves, you—you—you chili con carners?" The foreign-looking brethren looked hastily around, saw some Stadium policemen head their way, and made a quick exit, stuffing the handful of greenbacks they had been waving under Davis' and Pearson's noses, as they fled. Mrs. Manley slowly climbed back to her seat and sat there for two innings before the frown was completely erased from her furrowed brow.

June 25, 1947

"Major League 'Dozens' Playing"

I'll throw this one out and then duck. It's about the Ben Chapman—Jackie Robinson yow-yow. You know the situation in which Chapman, the

Phillies manager, told his charges to "ride" Jackie from the bench every chance they got and to do it with no holds barred. Ben, incidentally, is from Alabama, and wanted it laid on Jackie good and heavy, the explosive results of which brought words of wisdom from Commissioner Happy Chandler's office. Happy, you might recall, is a Kentuckian. Well, it seems that Chapman tried to explain to Dan Parker and the other scriveners who discovered the dastardly plot, that it was a prerogative of baseball big leaguers to "ride" everybody on an opposing team, and to "ride" them in any manner possible, including those that are legitimate.

Prior to 1947, such riding was confined to the racial distinctions whites were making among themselves. Thus, Italian players got it in the neck as did Irish and the few Jews who are in the majors. In other words, ballplayers played the "dozens" and made an art of it. The dozens, if you don't know what is meant by the term, can be played anywhere and heard anywhere, but Uptown and in the Harlems throughout the land, the "dozens" is an art and the practitioners are many and varied. The "dozens" then, is a manner of serious and derogatory discussion of ancestry with all the florid word extravaganzas of which one can conceive.

With Jackie Robinson in the majors, the complexion changed, and Ben Chapman was the first to publicly and openly decide that Robinson was suited for a baptism in the "dozens" as played by the major leaguers. Of course, "dozens" playing will get your head whipped in most circles, since few like disparaging remarks made about their parents by people they don't know. Now, the idea of putting Jackie in the major league "dozens" revolved mainly about his color, and it was there that Chapman hit on a splendid method of "riding" the Brooklyn Dodger first sacker. For a less handy person than Robinson, such "dozens" playing would be highly likely to be upsetting and might even bring about a clash if the equilibrium of the player in question is shaky. And Robinson's mental balance was supposed to be at the snapping point, what with all the responsibility shoved onto his shoulders. The Phillies opened on Jackie with all guns blazing and the logical response would have been for Jackie to run over to the Phillies' dugout and hit somebody in the jaw. He didn't, however, and Parker and others took up the matter and urged a stop before it got too far.

So widespread was public reaction to Chapman's program that Ben called it off, what with the front office hollering and the fans booing. Now, Chapman speaks up again, declaring that Robinson has not only made the major league grade, but was the principal figure in the Brooklyn drive toward a pennant. Said Ben: "He is a major leaguer in every respect. He can run, he can hit, he is fast, he is quick with the ball—and his fine base-running keeps the other team in an uproar."

You can write your own opinion about these remarks by Chapman. It might be pointed out that Ben is trying to get some of the publicity so richly given big Hank Greenberg, when he encouraged Jackie by identifying the Robinson attempt to make good with what he, Greenberg, had to take before he was accepted as a ballplayer. Chapman's opinion might be accepted tongue-in-the-cheek in light of what Ben had to say when he was busy siccing his players on Jackie and letting them put him in the "dozens" with impunity. However, in talking about the major league "dozens," it could be said that the emphasis laid on race and color and not ancestry, as might be the case where all Negro players were involved. The reason I'm pitching this up and getting set to duck, is that Chapman might be right after all. If they make fun of Greenberg, razzed the late Tony Lazzeri and made life holy hell for all racial stocks, why does Jackie have to exempted? Robinson is up there purely on his own.

The whole idea from the beginning was to divorce him from racial responsibilities and to allow him to sail on baseball's unchartered-for-a-Negro sea without strings attached. In such a condition, Robinson would necessarily run onto a lot of anti-black shoals. He ran into 'em in Florida when the Dodgers trained there. He encounters them in many places, and expects to run into many, many more.

I hold that one of the biggest obstacles to full participation by us in what benefits there may be under democracy, will be removed or reduced when we learn not to flinch at the word we all hate so thoroughly that others use to describe us and embarrass us. Yep, I mean the word, "nigger." Now, I'm the first to smack somebody in the kisser if they had the effrontery to call me one. So would you. But, that doesn't take away from the fact that the word has no power of itself to hurt. If we stopped letting it make us feel so badly or inferior, we would overcome a major barrier toward our advancement. Perhaps this isn't as clear as it should be. I'll try it from this angle: If a guy hits you, shoots you, refuses to let you in out of the rain or gets you put in jail, he's doing something tangible to hurt you. If he calls you out of name, as all of us frequently call one another, nothing is expended but the air used to form the words. If we worry too much over the air thus used, we can't play the game as in the case of Jackie.

Suppose Jack Johnson, when he was climbing toward the world heavyweight championship, had been deterred by what the fans, those in the boxing world and the newspapers, called him? And don't worry. They called him a thousand different kinds of you-know-what. But, Jack learned early what they called him didn't count. All that mattered was what happened once he got into the ring with 'em. And also, according to Jack, is how they paid off—a whole lot or a whole little. Sam Langford was called "The Boston Tarbaby," as a lot of old timers will recall, but that didn't keep him from being the terror of his day. Fritz Pollard was called a lot of you-know-what I'm talking about. So were Paul Robeson, Duke Slater, Rube Foster, Eddie Tolan, Sol Butler, Harry Wills, Charley West and others who were out there on the racial firing line in the early days of Negro participation in organized sports. While none of 'em liked being called you-know-what and while none would condone such descriptions, none have come up with scars to prove the word left then injured.

Unwittingly, Ben Chapman might have brought the problem out into the open, and to have centered the spotlight on a condition that should be attacked from another angle. Maybe, by his ordering of the Phillies to call Jackie Robinson such names, the proof has come out all the stronger that a mere word or term can't hurt, and also that the payoff is whether Robinson can run, field, hit, use his head and play ball like a major leaguer. The boys who are sure to follow Robinson in the big show will have to be big enough to shake off the discomfort at being called something they don't like, and to take such terms in stride, and to concentrate on being a great player, as in Robinson, and as are Greenberg, the Italians, the Poles, the Irish, the Germans, the Hungarians, the Czechs, the French, the Swedes, the Bohemians and others who have made baseball a racial polyglot of personalities, religion, race and background.

May 29, 1948

"The Local Story in Baseball"

They're playing consistently better baseball in the Negro National League in the local parks, but the people aren't coming out to see the games. Around 5,000 turned out last Sunday for the New York Cubans—Baltimore Elite Giants doubleheader at Yankee Stadium, a mere handful in light of what is needed to make the venture profitable.

The Cubans dropped both games—the first 3–2 and the second 9–6—for their first defeats at home, and it might be noted here that either club could whip Leo Durocher's Brooklyn Dodgers as of now, and might give many other major league clubs a run for their money. That's a lot to say, but when you look at the pitching on certain clubs in both the National and American Leagues, you get an idea of what I mean.

The Cubans have in Pat Scantlebury, a topflight lefty and the Baltimore club matches him with its Lefty Gaines. Were either white, they would be in major league livery and command respectable salaries.

Baltimore has in Henry Kimbro, bullet-sized outfielder, one of the best in baseball, both afield and at bat, as proved by him last winter when he won the batting championship of the Cuban Winter League. The league is inter-racial and has a lot of big name players.

The requirements of play are similar to those of the big leagues during the championship season, and Negro players usually acquaint themselves well. And you have to keep in mind this fact: that Negro players don't get the elaborate care in spring training and during the rest of the season that white players receive. They play the game from muscle and from a natural ability that springs from the fact that consistently, Negroes make better athletes than any other group. Yep, in boxing, football, baseball, basketball, and particularly in Negro baseball, these athletes need the support of the public.

It doesn't make you feel any good to see these fellows out there giving their all to stands three-quarters empty. You get to figure out what is taking place.

Around 400 players are involved in the Negro version of the national pastime, divided between the N.N.L. in the East and the N.A.L. in the West. They earn their living playing ball. If there are no customers out to see them, they don't earn a living.

It's as simple as that. A review of the economic pattern finds the same situation in the amusement world where people stay away from theaters and nightclubs, where they should go to keep a large segment of the race afloat.

In enriching the coffers of major league clubs, we put the cart before the horse for no purpose, save a matter of false pride and personal esteem that pays off in being able to brag, "I was there." Well, nobody saw him there or paid attention to his presence while at Yankee Stadium, the Polo Grounds or where ever else they might be playing a colored game. Yeah, it works out that way. Just like going to the Baptist Church on Sunday mornings, instead of the big white church in some other neighborhood. We've got to think these things out.

June 5, 1948

"Watching the Sports Parade"

It rained like hell over the weekend as you know, but they played baseball at both Ebbets Field and at Yankee Stadium on Monday, the day they made a holiday in honor of Memorial Day... But they didn't play at the Polo Grounds... Nearly 34,000 turned out for the afternoon game at Ebbets Field and 22,000 were on hand for the A.M. clash between the Giants and the Dodgers... A crowd of around 62,000 showed up at Yankee Stadium for the Washington Senators–Yankee embroglio... There might have been a fair turnout at the Polo Grounds, where the New York Cubans were scheduled to play the New York Black Yankees in a doubleheader, but from long experience, the fans knew that if even a cloud appeared overhead, they would call it off...

Truth of the matter is that the weight of the promotion is on one man, Alex Pompez, who owns the Cubans... Pompez has about lost his shirt this season promoting at the Stadium and the Polo Grounds... But, that is one of the ups and downs of sports promotion... You can ride a good one or get left at the post, but you've got to play the string out... Easiest thing in the world to lose right now is the loyalty of the few who want to see Negro baseball prosper... When they see the white leagues operating all around them, and then see a hesitancy or a complete failure to play ball by colored operators, they lose confidence and come to a surer opinion that the whole Negro baseball league business is nothing but a hoax...

If a game is scheduled and permission to play in the park has been obtained, the game should go on if there are but 50 people in the park... Many games have been played under those conditions, and fans over the years have come to have confidence in the operators and to support them on cloudy days as well as those where the sun bears down at a 90-degree clip... It was impossible to put on the Newark Eagles–Cubans twin bill Sunday... The rain that began Saturday night took care of that... But, the slight that disappeared as early as 1 P.M. Monday didn't preclude canceling the games completely, inconveniencing many people who were seen walking away from the Polo Grounds in disgust... They had made the trip there only to find out that they were wasting their time.

*   *   *

Jackie Robinson and Roy Campanella have the trail cleared ahead of them. Both can hit as well as play their positions with great versatility. Both are team players, a rare combination of talents, and in addition, they occupy the singular role of Negroes sparking the morals of white players.

*   *   *

Notice how Satchel Paige is getting along? White teammates are no novelty with this veteran of a thousand and one inter-racial contests. That's why Satchel, in the language of the fans, has been able to "blind 'em with his big foot thrown up in front of his delivery." Robinson has had white teammates in baseball, football, basketball and track, and thrives on it. Campanella had no trouble in adjusting himself because he comes of mixed parentage and has played the game with each and all.

ED HARRIS

A Brief Star

Ed Harris' star shone briefly in the sportswriting world. He covered sports for only a handful of years from the mid–1930s into the early 1940s, delighting *Philadelphia Tribune* readers with his solid grasp of baseball, a gentle sense of humor and droll observations on the world at large.

Harris was as apt to devote the paper's weekly sports column to his abiding love of pork chops or lifelong loathing of country picnics ("Picnics are well named; you pick bugs off you and nick your legs against briars, stones and other objects that dear Old Mother Nature has maliciously left in your way") as to various intricacies of the lineups for Hilldale or the Stars, Philadelphia's two best black baseball teams of the era.

Today at 80, Harris looks back with a kind of wry detachment on a sportswriting career that seemed to end as quickly as it started. After he left the sports beat, he spent a few years as city editor and then more than 20 years as the newspaper's managing editor. For him, the sports desk was a detour on the road to bigger things.

"I took the sports beat because that's what was offered me," Harris says. "I accepted the fact that sports was not really my bag. My interests were more whatever was going on—from city hall on down."

Yet Harris functioned alone much as did entire sport departments of other black weeklies of the era. "I was the sport department," the lifelong Philadelphia resident said. "As sports writer and editor, you were the one, and you did everything, from baseball to boxing, basketball and the Penn Relays."

Baseball was his favorite sport and the toughest to cover. "Associations with players were difficult because they were always on the road," Harris said of the game's barnstorming era. "You'd only see them occasionally, sit in the bullpen to chat, and the next thing you know, they were off on a bus going somewhere."

The *Tribune*'s tendency to shift writers around at a moment's notice may have been another problem. Harris wrote his sports column on and

Ed Harris (left) with Malcolm Poindexter of KYW-TV (photo courtesy Paris Gray and The Philadelphia Tribune*).*

off for three or four years, alternating with Randy Dixon and Jack Saunders. He left the sports beat for good in 1941, when he was named city editor and then managing editor. A short time later, he joined the army, fought in Europe and then came home to continue work at *The Tribune.*

Harris said he acquired his love of journalism from his aunt, the wife of Christopher Perry, who founded the *Tribune* in 1884 and served as its proprietor until 1921. After graduating from Central High School in 1931, Harris enrolled at the Temple University School of Journalism, but left after several semesters to work at the *Tribune.* He finished his degree at Temple in the mid–1940s, after returning from Europe.

"Perhaps the thing that sticks in my mind after all these years is not really about me, but about the others," he reflected in an interview. "People like Rollo Wilson and Wendell Smith knew their business, far better than I did. They were good; there's no getting away from it." For five years, though, Ed Harris was among the best sportswriters in the business.

April 11, 1935

"Satchel Can Do No Wrong"

Satchel Paige is causing his bosses out Pittsburgh way no end of trouble by failing to show up and report. By remaining incognito wherever he is, Satchel is only acting in keeping with that quaint and cute way of his of doing what he wants to do. Regardless of inconvenience to others, the Satchel is the Satchel.

His sweet and lovable character makes him respected and admired by his fellow players. You can tell that by the expression on their faces when ol' Satchel starts some more of his antics. And does the team morale perk up when the long-pedaled one starts acting up? Ask the club manager.

Guys like Paige may be interesting as the devil to the fans sitting in the grandstand. But to his teammates, he's usually a pain where you don't want to be kicked. The pet of the club owners is always giving somebody else a lot of trouble and getting away with it.

And they get away with it. Usually because they're good and know it, and the owner of the club knows it. Connie Mack had the same trouble with Rube Waddell, while other owners and managers have had similar trouble with the same type of player. Regardless of how good they might have been, there was always a tremendous sigh of relief when they passed from the picture.

Now, there's Satchel. Highest salaried man on his team and on a good many teams, his own car from the management—he can ride comfortably while the rest of the team goes by bus. Anything he wants is his and he takes it. But does that make him stop and appreciate his good fortune and act like a gentleman? It does not. Ol' Satch just goes off and does what Ol' Satch wants to do.

Is he ever wrong? Not that you would know it. Let one of his mates muff or fumble in a game that he is pitching. Did you ever hear the story of the King of France who came out of his palace to board a coach? The vehicle rumbled up just as the King stepped down the stairs. With a frown, he looked at the driver and said: "You almost made *me* wait." That, my friends, is the attitude Brother Satch takes. Temperament? The umpire who would call a decision on him would defy lightning. Walk off the field? Think nothing of it.

Of course, Satchel is an excellent pitcher. He can get away with that sort of stuff. But if I were manager of a club with him, either he would be boss or I would be the boss. There wouldn't be me or Satchel running the club. The effects of actions like that on the part of a player are far-reaching. The team as a whole suffers. They get that, "What's the use?" attitude.

The fans in the stands like it. It amuses them to see a grown man stamp his foot and rave like a three-year-old child. But it isn't good baseball and in the end, they get tired of it. Witness the case of Dizzy Dean, who figured he could run the Cards there for awhile. But when St. Louis Manager Frankie Frisch got through with him, there wasn't any use.

August 29, 1935

"At It Again"

(Very Special Editor's Note: Mr. Harris, who composed the following—we hesitate to classify it—has just returned from his vacation. His latest opus was written while he was still dizzy from dodging taxi cabs on Seventh Avenue, and the strain under which he was laboring is quite evident. So, if you read this, it's your own fault. Thank God we can say that all the ideas expressed and the manner used are solely and purely those of Mr. Harris.)

LAMENT ON THE EAST-WEST GAME

Oh beat the drums, buglers sound taps
While I recite of vile mishaps

That befell nine young men or more
Whose names you all have heard before.

The nine young men, baseballers true,
The Western team sought to subdue.

At Comiskey Park in the Windy City,
25,000 fans, hot and giddy

Pack the grandstands and the bleachers
To see what was one of the features

Of all the sports world yearly fare,
There were many more who wished they were there

Webster MacDonald of the Philly Stars
Headed the East team in the wars

The Western team was a very tough bunch
They were going to win, they had a hunch

The umpire screeched, "Come on, play ball,"
Then turned to the fans and said, "How you all?"

Slim Jones, the great, was at his best
But after the fourth had to take a rest

Dale went in and got a headache
And from the mound, Mac had him to take

Tiant went in and the Westerners scored
And MacDonald down the bullpen roared

To warm himself up and make the ball hum,
Cause he knew full well his time was come

He tossed a few and looked around
And there was Dihigo on the mound

He called time out but it was too late
Martin had burned one past the plate

Mac up and yells, "who put you here?"
The fans all said, "It's very queer."

He started to argue, but what's the use?
The boys had gone and cooked the goose

Mule Suttles was up, Oh fateful move
And Dihigo burned one down the groove

The bat met ball, the ball passed fence
And with it went the East team's chance

Turn back, oh time, but the deed is done
Mule Suttles' homer the game had won

And so my friends, Mac knows full well
That managing, like war, is hell.

August 6, 1936

"Abstract Reasoning"

The asininity of race prejudice, as practiced by the so-called "superior groups," is shown up by the feeble reasons advanced by its proponents for its existence. To the intelligent man, the theory of discrimination defeats itself by its own arguments.

In last week's issue, there was reprinted a column by Jimmy Powers, sports editor of the *New York Daily News,* in which he wrote about some of the letters he had gotten in relation to his favorable stand on Negro players in the big-leagues.

The pièce de résistance of the whole batch, came from a fan who raised the old familiar cry of *"Would you want your sister to marry one?"*

Now that, my friends, is a product of deep thinking, of a careful association of all the factors involved in the case and the resultant conclusion. Nothing but a brilliant man could have reached a decision whereby he felt that marriage and ball playing were related.

Powers triumphed, "No, but at the same time, I wouldn't want my sister to marry Bill Terry, Ty Cobb or Bill Klem, they're too grouchy." His reply was eminently correct and of a squelching variety.

Every objection recorded by Mr. Powers in his column could not be intelligently upheld. There was the usual cry that other ballplayers wouldn't associate with them, that fans in southern towns wouldn't stand for it, that Negro players were inherent gamblers and roisterers.

In my more or less frail association with big-league players in the American and National set-ups, it is my conclusion that very few of them spring from what might be termed "the best homes." In fact, as far as I'm concerned, quite a few of the boys could go down to Cat-gut Alley and not be noticed in mixing with the natives. The mass of ballplayers are like the mass of the American people, the very common and very ordinary. In company with them, quite a few Negroes might rightfully feel superior.

As for the conduct of fans in southern towns, it might be said that there are but few in the big leagues. Cincinnati, St. Louis and Washington are the towns. In Cincy and St. Louis, the sports' fans are used to seeing Negro athletes playing in company with whites. Quite a few of the football teams have had colored stars cavorting up and down the gridiron. I have yet to hear of any mob violence because some prejudiced white became infuriated at seeing a colored star play with the white boys.

As for Negroes being gamblers and roisterers, it would do some of the self-appointed critics good to view the behind-doors scenes when some of the big league boys get together in a quiet game of "bones" or poker. And the late, lamented Rube Waddell and the still-living but unfortunate Grover Cleveland Alexander never took any Sunday School prizes as models of propriety. The idol of present-day baseball, Babe Ruth, very nearly shut himself out of a manager's job by leaving behind him a history of irresponsibility and carefreeness.

The argument simply doesn't hold water.

The president of the National League, Ford Frick, put his stand in writing and said that except for ability, moral character and the like, there were no bans against any player in his league. This is all very ethical and abstract, but yet has nothing to do with Negro players, as Mr. Frick does not hire the athletes.

Some manager with guts and vision might precipitate things by signing up a colored player and seeing what would happen. It would clarify things a great deal. We would get some sort of decision, pro or con, instead of a lot of theories.

I have an idea that with the addition of Negro stars to the roster, that the turnstiles would start clicking regularly again. And I think that lots of baseball managers are of the same opinion. But baseball owners are notorious for their dislike of change. They like to hold onto the old things and not acquire newer methods. For instance, night ball. Cincinnati is the only team that has had the vision to install a light system and they have made money.

But, do the rest of the owners admit this? No. They bellow, "It is only a fad . . . It wouldn't last." That's what they said about the auto.

But, like all men, I live in hopes. Some day, someone will surprise the baseball world and sign a couple of good colored players. And the baseball world will be surprised to find out that after the initial interest and excitement, that the Negro will be accepted as part of the club and the world will go its way. Like lots of things, anticipation is much greater than realization.

September 24, 1936

"The Passing Show"

The people, John Fan and his brothers who support the different athletic events, are interesting creatures. Sit down sometime and ponder upon it and you will find that you have seen some mighty interesting persons watching a ballgame or a football tussle. Now, take the spectator at a baseball game.

The first type you are always to see is "the man who manages from the bleachers." Leave it to him and the pilot of a ball team isn't worth a dime a dozen. He sits up and informs his particular section where he is sitting, what the manager should have done. He loudly censures him when his decision has turned out wrong and has nothing to say but "I would have done that" when the pilot executes some brainy move. He has much to say about what the owner should do—he should hire this man, fire this one. He should do this, do that and so on. Many a small-minded soul fulfills a lifelong desire to be an executive by assuming a self-appointed role as "club manager."

Another type typical of the ballpark is the man "with an act." Maybe he can dance, or sing, or speak. But generally, all he has is a loud and rasping yell. He will yell anytime, at anything, for anyone. The first time he sounds off, the crowd laughs and cheers. The second time, the response is a little less enthusiastic. And as he continues his raucous rooting, the crowd gets more and more disgruntled as its annoyance increases. But, there is little to be done. He only shuts up when the game is over.

The fan "who gets excited" is perhaps the most interesting of all to watch. The game arouses his enthusiasm [so] that he loses control of himself and becomes a moving picture screen of what is happening on the diamond. If the team he is rooting for is losing, his face is black and low as clouds in a summer storm. If his team wins, his countenance beams forth sightly rays of hope and optimism. If strategy is needed, his mug looks like an apple that has been left in the corner. You need not to look on the field to see what is happening. Just keep your eye on his face. It will tell you all. And when it's over, he goes home happy, though he couldn't tell you so, because he has had a healthy, emotional release.

Then, there's the guy "who's mad." Ah, but he is a furious specimen. Suspicious of the moves of the other team and the umpires, he has his eyes open for any skullduggery. And let the first hint of it come to light and his mouth is open, his eyes blaze mighty wrath and he rises to defend his beloved team. His muscles bulge, his hair stands on end as he prepares to go to the aid of his beloved squad. Sometimes, he forgets himself and hits the umpire with a bottle. Another time, he insults a player and gets slugged in a fist fight. But, this is nothing to him. He remembers only one thing: "Eternal vigilance is the price of victory." And he's prepared to be on watch all the time. Fiery soul.

Another likely individual is the "peanut chewer." Peanuts are an integral part of any ballgame, but there are some who take their peanut chewing far too seriously. Take the chewer, who, through experience, has become a dilettante. He carefully and precisely cracks the peanut along the middle, casually drops half the shell to the floor and stamps on it, grinding it to bits in a meaty crackle. Then, he extracts the two peanuts from the other half and "pop," they go in his mouth. He chews thoughtfully and thoroughly until they have been properly masticated when he lowers his Adam's Apple and swallows. This done, and the peanut is in its proper place. He drops the other half of the shell and grinds it to dust. Satisfied that this particular peanut has been properly disposed of, he picks a likely looking victim from the bag and repeats the operation. And there being millions and millions of peanuts, the act goes on "ad infinitum."

The gentleman with the "long memory" is an institution. He remembers when everything happened. No matter how far your memory may extend, his always goes two or three years farther. This is all very disconcerting and annoying when you are trying to impress someone that you know something about the game. He remembers when so-and-so hit a homer and brought in eight runs, he knows what manager this-and-that said to player what's-his-name, when said player stole home and forgot there was a runner on third who stayed there. Sometimes, he even remembers so far back that it's wonderful until you remember that at the time he is speaking of, there were no ball teams.

Of course, the fellow who "knows the players personally" must be recalled. Listen to him and he's bosom pals with the ballplayers on every club in the league. He will tell you what Catcher Brown had to say to him about the running of the team and what Outfielder Page thought when he told him of the plan to win games; without him, the players would be orphans in the country. He shouts and waves greetings to them as they walk down the field and is immensely gratified when the player, wondering where all that noise is coming from, feebly waves in return. When they meet him on the street, he loudly hurls a greeting and is tickled pink when he gets an uncertain "hello." This, to him, is manna. Meanwhile, the ballplayer is walking down the street and wondering what taproom the guy lives in.

Of course, there is the fellow who "gets in with a pass." Just take all the fellows I have outlined, double their particular qualities, and the fellow with the Annie Oakley has them.

April 22, 1937

"An Amazing Parallel"

There is something of a parallel in the present status of two league teams in Philadelphia, namely, the Philadelphia Athletics and the Philadelphia Stars. Maybe a bit farfetched a comparison, but we won't go into that.

The Athletics are owned partly, and managed by Connie Mack, one of the pioneers of organized baseball. The Stars are supervised by Ed Bolden, without doubt a stalwart of Negro baseball from way back.

But the parallel I'm most interested in drawing is that this year, both teams are going to try to make it off rookies and it can't be done.

The Athletics are loaded to the gills with first-year aspirants who will be making initial appearances. All of Connie Mack's wisdom will not give them the knowledge that only experience will bestow upon them.

Ed Bolden will have a similarly hard job.

The Stars need new faces, but it would have been far better strategy for the management to have tried to get one or two of the better known veterans who were still in their prime. It could have been done. For one,

Dick Seay would have returned and no one need tell you that Dick was always a popular player in these parts.

The veterans on the team, aside from having been known to the fans for many, many years, are fast approaching the point where they won't be able to do the things they did in days gone by. With all respect in the world for them and their past records, there is no way on earth that they can expect to achieve the heights of days gone by.

Ed Bolden sees this and is going to try to replace or assist the vets with virgin rookies. That may turn out or it probably won't. Rookies are all right in their places, but their places are not in the firing line day after day in the heat of a pennant fight. It's a good way to get experience, but that experience will be purchased at the cost of many wins.

Then again, there's the box office angle. Nobody loves a loser and damn few will go to see one. But given a hustling and fighting ballclub that annexes its share of wins, and the Philadelpia fans will go nuts for them and travel in many crowds to see the team.

But it is unreasonable to expect that the local collection of bleacherites will pay their hard-earned cash to see a bunch of hapless rookies in action. Saving only one contingency and that is by some miracle the rookies being transported north by Mr. Bolden turn out to be instant "killers." If this is so, then Mr. Bolden is thrice blessed and is a very lucky man.

But I am sore afraid that the coming season will find Mr. Bolden and his cohort, Jud Wilson, of the fiery temper, doing some tall scuffling to turn out a winning ballclub. I hope they can do it 'cause I'd hate to see the parallel between the A's and the Stars extended to the point that, like the A's, the Stars would be chosen to finish in last place.

August 4, 1938

"Judge Landis Gives a Lesson in Decency and Good Sense"

Mr. Jake Powell of the New York Yankees got something of a lesson last weekend out Chicago way.

In a radio interview over a local station, Jake was asked what he did in the winter.

Thereupon, the outfielder replied that he was a policeman in his hometown of Chicago and kept in batting trim by using his club "on niggers."

Thereupon, Mr. Powell was cut off the air.

Several things proceeded to happen.

Complaints and demands for apologies began flooding the offices of the radio station. The station broadcast six separate apologies that evening.

Judge Landis suspended Powell for 10 days, right in the midst of the Yankees' drive for pennant honors, and at a time when all first-string players were needed in the field.

A movement was started by Southside Negroes to have Powell make a public apology for his remarks.

Which no doubt, gives Jake Powell much thought in his 10 days' exile. He'll probably learn to keep his mouth shut after this.

The Yankees and the players on other teams have got a good lesson in just what decency and a sense of non-prejudice is worth. By the hard way—the cash box.

I hope we can get a lesson from it.

August 18, 1938

"Our Jud"

Who is this ambling to the plate,
Bow legs a'rocking side to side?
It's mighty Jud (Wilson), our heart's delight,
To take a crack at the horsehide

With heavy bat and muscles strong,
Determination on his face,
He tips his hat and takes his stand,
The cheers are rocking this old place.

Whenever there's another run
The Stars need to tie the score,
We know that when Boojum's up,
The hit will come and maybe more.

Maybe at first he's nit too lithe
At reaching for a scorching ball,
But when it comes to knocking out the pill,
Why Jud can take them all.

And if a player starts to lag
And lets defeat his playing mar,
Who is it who'll be at his side,
And have him acting like a Star?

Why Jud, of course. A million things.
Boojum can do to make the team
A classy bunch of ballplayers
That gives the Chief reason to beam.

Say what you will for youngsters bright
Who come along to take the place
Of older men, who've seen their day.
It takes some years to make an ace.

The things a good ballplayer learns,
Are not picked up in just one day.
Through many years he lessons gets
And for them, he has to pay.

And ball games are not always won
By heavy hitters, classy throws,
A lot of thinking can help out
And here you need someone who knows.

So Boojum fills the spot round here,
Results—the Stars do have some style,
The younger ones supply the hits
And Jud Wilson supplies the guile.

May 16, 1940

"Mr. Fan Is Ready—But Is Baseball?"

That Negro baseball is still a paying proposition was amply demonstrated by two openings of league teams so far this season.

Here in the Quaker City, the Philadelphia Stars premiered with the Elite Giants Saturday at 44th and Parkside to a full house, almost 5,000 persons who were willing to put down their cash to see the colored boys in action.

Comparatively speaking, this is a larger crowd than the Athletics or the Phillies had on hand when their major league seasons began.

The previous Sunday saw Newark blowing its top with what must have been the largest opening day crowd ever seen in Negro baseball.

More than 12,000 persons were on hand when the Eagles faced the New York Black Yankees. This was all cash and most of it in the grandstand of the park used by the Newark Bears, the Yankees' minor loop club.

There were added attractions, but none so popular that such a crowd would be attracted solely by them. Boxer Henry Armstrong threw out the first ball, and Runners John Borican and Herbert Thompson were in the boxes, guests of Mr. and Mrs. Manley, the club owners. Other celebrities and dignitaries were on hand. But there was no getting away from the fact that it was baseball and colored baseball that drew this large crowd. It even seemed like the old times when spectators in the stands raced to the edge of the field to give dollar bills to different players for some spectacular bit of work.

*   *   *

This Sunday will see the Yanks and the Cubans starting off in Yankee Stadium with the lieutenant governor of the state of New York on hand to do the honors.

Naturally, no one expects that opening day crowds will persist throughout the season, but it is safe to say that a potential strong and consistent following is embodied in the spectators, who swarm to see the first of the season.

Yet, there is always a flaw.

Here in Philadelphia, the game turned out to be a shabby affair, long drawn out and boring toward the end, even when the Stars came near to pushing ahead in a Merriwell finish. The Boldenmen showed a sorry lack of coherence, and once more, it was pointedly revealed that not for nothing do the big league clubs go South in the winter. A team can't get into mid-season form by playing two or three sets of doubleheaders before its league season begins. Whatever the Stars will be in another month's time, they are still a long way from it.

*   *   *

Up in Newark, one who would have gazed about the stands and the spectators seated therein, would have seen 95 colored faces for every five white ones. The game was promoted and ballyhooed through Negro sources and to Negro people. Yet, the Eagles' management has the temerity to hire a white press agent to do their work, and who is lucky is he is able to get two-or-three column inches of copy in one of the white dailies. That the Manleys are free to do what they will with their teams is to be admitted — but, it doesn't add up right when you consider their attitude toward Eddie Gottlieb and his connections with the Philadelphia Stars.

So it goes, another season has started and the league is again on its way.

Whether springing or limping along, it somehow gets to the end of its appointed round, and thus, despite all the mistakes and errors of owner, player and spectator, it reveals the basic strength of the game and the power and hold it has in the public mind.

August 7, 1941

"Nine Years Old, 50,000 Big"

You read about the 50,000 persons who saw the East-West game and the thousands who were turned away from the classic, and you get to wondering what the magnates of the American and National leagues thought about it when they read the figures.

Did any of them feel a faint stir in their hearts, a wish that they could use some of the many stars who saw action to corral some of the coin evidently interested in them?

Or did they, hearing the jingling of the turnstiles in this, one of the good seasons baseball has had, just dismiss the motion and reserve the idea of Negro players in the big leagues until the next time there is a depression and baseball profits begin to decline?

Fifty thousand people at any baseball game, World Series included, is no small figure. The All-Star Game didn't draw half that number, and there will be few games this season that will draw 50,000.

Personally, I don't think that the 50,000 people present will have any effect whatsoever on the minds of those who are for or against the Negro in baseball. They are convinced already. Those who are for it and those who are against it would admit, if you could pin them down, that there is a real financial golden goose in the proposition. They know it already; they don't need to be told.

But those who don't want to see the colored man playing big league ball don't want to see him because he's colored. He could bring an increase of $25,000 to the team in a season and he still won't be wanted. So, 50,000 at the East-West Game won't mean much one way or the other.

*   *   *

But, it is a triumph for Negroes. It is one of the soundest evidences of the community spirit in the Midwest. You could hold the East-West game in the East for the next 10 years and you wouldn't have the attendance that the Midwest will have in five.

Say what you will about Chicago and Detroit and the other big towns out that way being away from the places where "things happen." You'll have to admit the fact that colored people really know how to live.

Blasé New York, with its "Living in Harlem is the only thing," and staid Philadelphia, with its self-satisfaction, won't ever make the progress racially that the new up-and-doing communities of the West are.

There have been all-star games here and in New York, where Yankee Stadium, one of the finest parks in the country, was available. The Stadium and the Polo Grounds aren't five minutes' car ride from the heart of Harlem, but do you think 50,000 people got that far? I won't wait for an answer.

So, Chicago can take a bow or a couple of bows. The boys who played ball can bow also that they have the stuff to attract that many people. The Negro American and National leagues can take a bow for having thought up the attraction, though they are being well-paid for their investment. The boys really cut a melon, not a lemon.

INDEX